OBAMA POWER

To the memory of Iwan and Nadja Jaworsky
And the future memories of Ben and Kia, Aaron and Sylvia

OBAMA POWER

Jeffrey C. Alexander and
Bernadette N. Jaworsky

polity

First published in 2014 by Polity Press

Polity Press
65 Bridge Street
Cambridge CB2 1UR, UK

Polity Press
350 Main Street
Malden, MA 02148, USA

ISBN-13: 978-0-7456-8199-3
ISBN-13: 978-0-7456-9662-1 (pb)

A catalogue record for this book is available from the British Library.

Typeset in 10.25 on 14 pt Sabon
by Servis Filmsetting Ltd, Stockport, Cheshire
Printed and bound in the US by Edwards Brothers, Inc.

The publisher has used its best endeavours to ensure that the URLs for external websites referred to in this book are correct and active at the time of going to press. However, the publisher has no responsibility for the websites and can make no guarantee that a site will remain live or that the content is or will remain appropriate.

Every effort has been made to trace all copyright holders, but if any have been inadvertently overlooked the publisher will be pleased to include any necessary credits in any subsequent reprint or edition.

For further information on Polity, visit our website: www.politybooks.com

Contents

Preface

This book is not about the exercise of Obama power during the Democratic president's second term in office, but about what gave him the opportunity to do so – his odds-defying victory in the 2012 presidential campaign. Obama's party had suffered horrendous defeat in the mid-term elections just two years earlier, his poll ratings had tanked, and the bloom was off the Obama rose. If these downward trends had continued, the world, at least the American world, would look very different today. Mitt Romney would be president, tax cuts for the wealthy would have been deepened rather than reversed, conservative hegemony over the Supreme Court would have been set for another generation, and new wounds to the already fragile social welfare safety net would have been suffered. It is sometimes difficult to remember such "what ifs," given the continuing paralysis and deeply frustrating polarizations that have thus far rained over Obama's second reign. But it is not a bad thing to recall them, for they were just barely avoided. The "what ifs" (about Romney being elected) would have been replaced by the "what might have beens" (about an Obama second term).

To find out why Obama won, this book drills down to the bedrock of US politics and culture. We examine the texture of American life, employing a microscope instead of a telescope, taking a granular view. When it comes to electoral outcomes, long views and big pictures are really views from nowhere. Searching for the deep underlying causes of the Democratic victory is like reading tea leaves – it's not much more than making things up. Was it the ebb and flow of the economy, the surging shifts of demography, the formation of a new progressive ideology? Did Obama's victory crystallize a new electoral coalition? Did Romney's defeat mark the end of right-wing conservatism and the reinvigoration of the welfare state? Has the 30-year neo-conservative wave finally crested? Such grand issues were neither cause nor consequence of Obama's victory and Romney's defeat. They do not cut close enough to the bone. In what follows, we are interested not in structures but in processes. Not the why but the how. We offer a new interpretation of US politics in the critical four years from January 2009 to November 2012.

We are extraordinarily grateful to John Thompson, editor and publisher of Polity Press, for providing critical support and feedback for this project from its beginning as a series of public lectures through its various manuscript lives. We also thank Jason Mast, Roger Friedland, and Ballard Morton for editorial responses to the manuscript at critical points. Alexander wishes to express his gratitude to the University of Cambridge, where he was in residence during the writing of this book, as the 2012–13 Pitt Professor of American History and Institutions while on sabbatical from Yale University. Jaworsky thanks her colleagues and students at Masaryk University in Brno, the Czech Republic, where her research was supported under a grant for the Employment of Newly Graduated Doctors of Science for Scientific Excellence (CZ.1.07/2.3.00/30.0009), co-financed from the European Social Fund and the state budget of the Czech Republic.

"The great intellectual advantage of telling stories is that it does not rationalize the irrationality of actual experience and of history."
Judith N. Shklar, *Ordinary Vices*

Introduction

In 2008, Barack Obama not only became the first African American to be elected president of the United States but the most vivid symbol of America's democratic aspirations in decades. These utopian hopes proved hard to fulfill. Despite some remarkable legislative achievements, Obama's popularity soon went into free fall, and his Democratic Party was humiliated in the midterm elections of November 2010. Over the next two years, the tides reversed again, and President Obama won a sweeping re-election victory over the Republican Mitt Romney in November 2012.

This book is about the deflation and re-inflation of a political symbol – "Barack Obama" – from 2009, the beginning of Obama's first term in office, to his re-election in 2012. The odds were strongly against the Democratic president's re-election. It was not just that his popularity had sunk to dangerous depths. It was also that the Supreme Court had removed controls over corporate campaign donations and unemployment had soared to a height that had prevented any previous sitting president since FDR from being re-elected. Yet, while such material issues create high hurdles, they can be overcome. Whether Obama would be re-elected or shoved aside by Mitt Romney was an open question. It was decided neither by economy nor by demography, as important as both of these were. What was decisive was Obama's ability to make meaning – to become a powerful political symbol – and Romney's inability in turn.

Cultural symbols and dramatic performances determined the fate of Obama's presidency. For political performances to be successful, they must connect, or "fuse," with large segments of the citizenry that compose their audience. If this connection is effected, then what might be called the performative dimension of politics – not only the candidates' feigning truthfulness, but the speech writers, advertisers, make-up artists, advance men, spinners, and fundraisers who devote themselves to molding their images – becomes invisible to the naked eye. The candidate seems natural. But when performance and reception are not welded together, the seams show; political action seems contrived and overtly "performative" – strategic, mechanical, inauthentic. The premise of this book is that citizens don't rationally deliberate the "real" qualities of candidates so much as they experience emotionally their projected moral tone.

Political elections have a real, very objective goal. They are all about winning and taking control of the government. In democratic societies, however, struggles for state power must be played out in non-violent ways. Democratic politicians take great pains to demonstrate their civility even as they engage in the fiercest of competitions. The premise of civility is that we are all in this together, that we are members of a "civil sphere" and not just an economic or political sphere, a religious order or an ethnic regime. A broadly *civil* solidarity undergirds the democratic state – that, at least, is the utopian idea. That we are a moral and not only a legal community, that we feel solidarity and trust with one another despite our differences and conflicts – this is the conceit that makes democracy possible.

In electoral struggles, this civility and the moral community it makes possible are at issue. Candidates compete with one another over who can embody democratic morality and sustain solidarity, and who cannot. This is trickier than it seems, because political morality is Janus-faced. It's about not only the civil good but also anti-civil evil. It aims to separate honesty from deceit and altruism from selfishness, and to protect free people from despotism. The performance of politics is about wrapping yourself in the bright canopy of democratic values and painting your opponent in darkly anti-democratic colors.

Political campaigning tells a story about purity and pollution, about who is qualified to protect and extend solidarity and who would narrow and endanger it. To be associated with "anti-civil" qualities is to be symbolically constructed as immoral. Electing such a polluted figure would threaten the solidarity upon which democracy depends. Successful political performers plant their feet squarely inside the civil sphere. Demonstrating their moral trustworthiness, they work furiously to push their opponents outside the world of civility into the immoral world outside.[1]

1

The Performance of Politics

On November 2, 2010, when the Democratic Party suffered severe defeat at the hands of its Republican opponents, 63 seats turned over in the House of Representatives, the most in a midterm election since 1938. Democrats gave up control of this major legislative body to a new Republican majority. They also lost critical seats in the government's other legislative body, the Senate, maintaining control only by a thin margin.

These bare-faced facts were interpreted by the mass media in dramatic terms, as "The Death of the Hero." In the days leading up to the election, Maureen Dowd, an influential syndicated columnist for the *New York Times*, had prophesied about the president's "coalition and governing majority shattering around him."[1] A poll taken among 18–24-year-old students just two weeks prior declared that the "Obamamania that gripped college campuses two years ago is gone."[2] Even Hollywood liberals were quiet during the last push, reflecting an "enthusiasm gap."[3]

The day after the defeat, the *New York Times* posted an ominous, almost Shakespearean headline: "In Republican Victories, Tide Turns Starkly."[4] The *Wall Street Journal* spoke of the "balkanized state of American politics" after the "historic" election,[5] and its conservative opinion editor rejoiced, "The Empire Strikes Back ... Let the recriminations begin!"[6]

The conservative *Washington Examiner*'s Byron York predicted "irreconcilable conflict."[7] The *New Yorker*'s senior
editor, former Jimmy Carter speech writer Hendrik Hertzberg,
augured: "For him and for the country, the next two years look
awfully bleak. Capitol Hill will be like Hamburger Hill, a noisy
wasteland of sanguinary stalemate."[8]

There was blood in the water, a smell of murder in the air.
Right-wing activists from the "Tea Party" had risen to power
and challenged the status quo among the GOP. "Not since Barry
Goldwater thumbed his nose at country-club Republicans in
1964 has a rebel movement created such a crisis of legitimacy
among the GOP establishment," proclaimed *TIME*.[9] After
the elections, the Republicans welcomed its new right-wing
members into the legislative ranks. As then House speaker-in-
waiting John Boehner put it: "What unites us as Republicans
will be the agenda of the American people."[10] Obama's rise
had not heralded the rebirth of liberalism, but merely a tem-
porary zig-zag on the long and steady horizon of conservative ascendancy. With the defeat of Obama's party in 2010,
the line had now been straightened back out. "Today the
American people admitted the mistakes they made two years
ago," one of the founders of the group, the Tea Party Patriots,
declared.[11] "Personally, I think he's already lost his re-election,"
Dick Armey trumpeted triumphantly about the president.[12]
The neo-conservative activist and former Bush cabinet secretary had been the leading establishment figure behind the Tea
Party's confrontation with Barack Obama's healthcare plan in
the summer of 2009.

America's conservative pundits interpreted the massive
Republican shift as the rebuking response of the US electorate to a leftist president, one whose government-directed programs of redistribution stretched from Wall Street regulation
to the auto industry bailout and healthcare reform. Republican
master strategist Karl Rove described voters as "sick of the

administration's direction and tone" and accused the president of embracing a blame-game attitude "creating a vast army of people who feel personally assaulted by him."[13] John Boehner declared: "The American people have sent an unmistakable message to him [the president] tonight and that message is 'change course'!"[14] On Fox News, former Alaska governor and vice-presidential candidate Sarah Palin offered some advice to the president going forward: "He is the one who is going to have start coming more to the center of America, toward some middle ground, instead of staying on that extreme far left that has driven us to where we are today."[15] In its end-of-year editorial for 2010, the Rupert Murdoch-owned *Wall Street Journal* could scarcely conceal its satisfaction. The election result, it opined, was a clear-eyed, up and down judgment by rational citizens about liberal social policies: "The real story of 2010 is that the voters were finally able to see and judge this liberal agenda in its unvarnished form."[16]

These statements about the meaning of the 2010 election, however, were less reflections of social reality than efforts to shape it. Forcefully crystallizing hopes and fears, they were interpretations of the voting result, not objective descriptions of it. Rather than denoting a condition that already exists, they constituted efforts to bring that condition into being by the very action of speaking about it. They were, in other words, political performances.

Is the electorate really rational in the way that reactions to the Democrats' 2010 defeat suggested? Are the opinions of voters really so clear? How do we know what a vote indicates, exactly? Can we even speak of an "electorate" per se? Is it empirically correct that the results of the 2010 congressional voting actually indicated something about an entity called "the American people"?

From a cultural perspective, voting is viewed as symbolic communication, a political performance that demands interpretation. No doubt, those who participated in the election, and those who didn't, were reacting to something about President Obama's first two years in office, but was it, in fact, the leftist nature of his policies? Was the Republican shift in voting perhaps less a clear-eyed citizenry responding to liberal policies than a response to a symbolic failure – the weakness of his performance of liberal politics? Perhaps it reflected this liberal administration's inability to reach out to centrist audiences and the clumsy inadequacy of its efforts to get even potentially sympathetic audiences emotionally engaged.

Leaders do not offer policy to clear-eyed citizens who rationally evaluate its effectiveness and register their deliberative judgment through their votes. Political leaders project complex and multilayered performances to audiences who engage these symbolic actions with more and less enthusiasm, with more and less criticism, and may not actually engage with them at all. Strictly speaking, such responses are not even interpretations of political actions. What citizens have available to them is only "news" about these actions – only journalistic reconstructions. What voters interpret are mass-mediated performances.

In the 2010 exit polls, only 37 percent of those casting votes – for their local congressional representatives – viewed the national election as a referendum on the Obama administration. Another 24 per cent did not. The remaining 39 percent of the electorate were not sure how to interpret the vote.[17]

And what about those who had not voted? Significant segments of the aroused electorate that had thrust Obama into power during the presidential voting in 2008 sat out the midterm congressional election two years later.[18] Polls indicated that the audience of young voters aged 18–29, the so-called youth vote, continued to favor Obama by an historically unprecedented majority.[19] In 2010, however, relatively few of these young voters cast their votes – just 11 percent, compared to 18 percent in 2008.[20] Despite the even deeper and wider commitment of

African Americans to Obama, their participation in November 2010 declined as well. Just 25 percent had given "quite a lot of" or "some" thought to the midterm elections, compared to 44 percent in 2006 and 85 percent in the 2008 presidential elections.[21] One black commentator observed a few days before the election: "[T]he sense of hope and history that drove turnout in 2008 are in short supply."[22]

The exercise of political power is not only pragmatic and practical, but cultural – not just about getting things done, but about making legislative accomplishments and organizational changes seem meaningful and legitimate. The electorate responds to the manner and style of power. President Obama had been a powerful executive in purely pragmatic terms, initiating far-reaching repairs that would deeply alter the social organization of American society. In the process of accomplishing these organizational reforms, however, he had been unable to make meaning in his old way. He lost his symbolic footing. His actions, while effective legislatively, were no longer affecting. As the president's performances lost symbolic power, the Tea Party rose up and unceremoniously kicked the once and future American hero off the public stage. "The buzz and intensity for some months now has been on the right, led by the Tea Party," the *New York Times* observed in March, 2010.[23] After the midterm elections, seven out of ten Americans felt that it was very or somewhat important that "Republican leaders in Congress take the Tea Party movement's positions and objectives into account as they address the nation's problems."[24]

The venerable political journalist Elizabeth Drew observed in the leftist *New York Review of Books*: "President Obama seems to be shrinking and becoming more ineffectual before our eyes."[25] The Democratic defeat in 2010 was a reflection of this cultural deficit. In the wake of the deflation of their party's political symbol, Democratic political campaigners had tried to "reignite"[26] the audiences of citizens who had supported them in 2008, but they could not generate the spark. The Democrats had been looking for a way to "energize" the electorate,[27] but they could not find it.

This book describes the symbolic deflation of Obama's early years in office and explains how the Democratic president eventually found a way to get his mojo working again. We show how it was the cultural re-inflation of "Obama power" – not only shifting demographic and economic indicators – that allowed the Democratic Party to gain traction and the liberal president to be elected again.[28]

2

Symbolic Deflation

In his campaign for the presidency in 2008, Barack Obama had delivered a striking performance that powerfully connected with the left and the center sections of the citizenry, even as it deeply antagonized the right. He deftly deployed the moral language that undergirds US democracy and, demanding "change we can believe in," presented himself as a transformative figure, a singular political hero who would solve the crisis of our times and take the nation along a new path.

Performing as a successful president, however, is even more difficult – exponentially more so – than winning the campaign. In one sense, the challenge is the same – to become a collective representation of democratic ideals. But the social circumstances surrounding this cultural effort have starkly changed. Political campaigns can be conducted in the future tense; presidents, by contrast, must tell their stories in real time. It is much more difficult to tell your story when you need to account for a real situation, especially when your position as head of state makes contemporary social conditions seem your responsibility.

The first two years of Obama's presidency, 2009 and 2010, unfolded as a sequence of political duels that amounted to vicious, if symbolic, knife fights. Each side invoked the dichotomies of democratic morality to do maximum cultural injury to the other: Who is secretive, who open? Who is truthful and reasonable, who deceptive and domineering? Who is trying to be cooperative and who aggressive and bullying? Whose policies constitute a threat to the autonomy of individuals on the other side?

Healthcare as Primal Scene

The primal scene was the battle over healthcare reform. Republicans accused the administration and its liberal representatives of dishing out phony numbers and making secret deals. They highlighted the Obama administration's insistence on the so-called "mandate." Every American would be required to purchase health insurance, or else to pay a substantial fine. Since Teddy Roosevelt had first proposed government-sponsored healthcare a century before, American resistance to "socialized medicine" was legendary. Controversy over the mandate triggered deep moral anxieties about individual submission to an impersonal, domineering, and bureaucratic state.

What emerged was a melodrama featuring the very public struggle between grass-roots "Tea Party" activists and an Obama-led, full court press for major government legislation. For the right, that push had all the earmarks of an anti-democratic conspiracy. During the summer congressional recess in 2009, just months into Obama's first term, right-wing activists began to stage an extraordinarily effective symbolic struggle against the healthcare proposal. Dressed in the garb of the eighteenth-century American colonists who protested King George's luxury taxes and triggered the Revolution, the Tea Party movement exploded on the scene, grabbing the headlines in newspapers and television. Announcing "Beyond Beltway, Health Debate Turns Hostile," the *New York Times* reported on the "volatile mix" of heckling and even violence when Tea Party members protested at town-hall meetings held by congressional members across the country during the 2009 summer break.[1]

Reporting on the largest of these rallies, held on September 12, Fox News declared "Tea Party Express Takes Washington By Storm," noting that "tens of thousands" of protestors were chanting, "enough, enough" and "you lie, you lie!"[2]

While they were far from monolithic, Tea Party activists were united in their effort to block the Patients Protection and Affordable Care Act, which many dubbed "Obamacare," from becoming law.[3] They repeatedly portrayed Obama as a socialist, in their view the radical obverse of American-style democracy.[4] When Jenny Beth Martin, the national Tea Party Patriots coordinator, enumerated the movement's "core principles," she equated "fiscally responsible" officials with "constitutionally limited government" and "free markets."[5] The sacred democratic code of individual autonomy was interpreted as demanding non-interference by government: "There are two competing visions for health care in America. One centralizes control in Washington DC, while the other empowers families and individuals – i.e. the patients."[6]

As the healthcare debate heated up, *Newsweek* headlined, "The Case for Killing Granny."[7] A big "bogeyman," as one Dartmouth Medical School professor called it, was the idea that somehow care for the elderly could become rationed. Former Alaska governor and vide-presidential candidate Sarah Palin stoked the fire by referring to "death panels" of bureaucrats that would decide who was "worthy of healthcare." Her comments propelled an enormous push to code the health reform as deeply immoral, a danger to democratic civility; indeed, Palin called the proposal "downright evil."[8] This death panel metaphor, and the media interpretations layered on top of it, was to prove remarkably durable. Even two years after the Act was passed, four in ten Americans still believed the law would create death panels.[9]

Obama's response to this pressing pollution was to reach for symbolic representations of his own that would resonate with the center of the citizen audience. In a town-hall meeting in Colorado, he invoked Social Security, the most popular and taken-for-granted governmental benefit, reminding the audience that opponents had called it socialist when President Franklin Roosevelt had first introduced the idea in the 1930s.[10] A few days later, the Democratic president tried tapping into what he called the "moral convictions" of religious organizations. Proclaiming that the healthcare debate "goes to the heart of who we are in America," he asserted the "core ethical and moral obligation that we look after each other."[11] He was translating the widely popular Medicare program for older Americans into the moral language that sustains social solidarity, calling it a "sacred trust that must be passed from generation to generation."[12]

But regardless of how energetically Obama projected such rhetoric into the court of public opinion, these performances did not connect with the hearts of the US audience. It was not that the president failed in practical terms. Eventually, the Act was passed into law, and repairs to the inequitable and costly state of American healthcare were begun. In symbolic terms, however, tremendous damage had been done to Obama's cultural power. Not a single Republican in the House or Senate voted for the bill. Public opinion on the issue shifted considerably, not toward but away from the president's side. In June 2009, most Americans (72 percent) supported the idea of a "government administered health plan like Medicare that would compete with private health insurance plans," and 57 percent said they would be willing to pay higher taxes so that all Americans would have coverage they couldn't lose "no matter what."[13] But by the time the Act became law, in March 2010, only 32 percent approved of it.[14]

Obama had won the battle but lost the war. He proved unable to energize the feelings of solidarity that are necessary to legitimate egalitarian institutional change. It was the

ceremonial powers of the office that were at stake. As compared
with Britain, where the Crown and Prime Minister are starkly
separated, in America the same person, the president, exercises
both instrumental and symbolic power. As the King (or Queen)
of the civil sphere, a president carries not only a legal mandate
but what the ancient Chinese called the mandate of heaven. He
is not just the head of government, but the guarantor of social
peace and tranquility; there are ruffles and flourishes, standing
and deference, wherever he goes. Describing the "hushed crowd
of 1.5 million" listening to President Obama's 2009 inauguration speech, *People* magazine made note of the promise he
made to the assembled faithful: "We have gathered because
we have chosen hope over fear, unity of purpose over conflict
and discord."[15] Hope and unity were precisely what President
Obama had been unable to sustain.

This ceremonial function of the presidency is such that, if
partisanship increases, the mandate of heaven may be considered lost. If there is political paralysis and venomous, seemingly
endless bickering, the president can become vulnerable indeed.
If civility seems endangered, then it is harder for the president
to present himself as a symbol of the entire nation. The ide-
alized solidarity required for legitimating radical institutional
change breaks down.

This same deflation of authority afflicted the presidencies
of Obama's predecessors. The symbolic power of Kennedy,
Johnson, Nixon, Clinton, both Bushes, and even Reagan had
withered in the face of intense partisanship and political paralysis. But Obama was particularly vulnerable because of the hero
story he represented. The persona he had constructed promised
to create a new vital center, to lead the nation beyond the polar-
ization of the 1960s generation, to unity and consensus over
conflict and discord. This hero narrative, paradoxically, gave
the Republican opposition veto power over Obama's success.
They deployed this cultural power with ruthless magnificence.

If they erupted in endless partisanship, and refused to compromise, it would appear, symbolically speaking, to be Obama's own fault. He had not fulfilled his responsibility as president to create a civil society. He had lost the mandate of heaven and fallen from grace.

The Economy and National Mood

Partisan political eruption was the first social fact that undermined Obama's symbolic authority during this first term. The failure of the economy to dramatically improve was the other. The economy is politically significant not only because it affects the material situation of a decisive segment of the voting populace, but also because the state of the economy creates a mood, establishing a tonality in the collective conscience that affects everybody. The economy delivers cultural as well as material goods – the hopes and anxieties that affect what Keynes called capitalism's "animal spirits." These moods and emotions translate into estimations of the president's civil capacities. "It's so psychological," the *Wall Street Journal*'s "MarketWatch" would explain in the midst of the 2012 race, asserting that voters' "gut feeling" would ultimately decide their vote.[16]

Candidate Obama promised that, if elected, he would resolve the economic crisis. President Obama, in the early days of his first term, predicted that, if his nearly trillion-dollar stimulus package were passed, unemployment would stand at 6 percent four years later, by next Election Day. He painted a forward-moving narrative of economic salvation: "I have every confidence that if we are willing to continue doing the critical work that must be done – by each of us, by all of us – then we will leave this struggling economy behind us, and come out on the other side, more prosperous as a people."[17] But in the early years of his presidency, the economy moved in the wrong direction, from an unemployment rate of 7.8 percent when he took office to 9.5 percent by the 2010 midterm election, even rising to 10 percent in late 2009.[18]

Some critics, including the future Republican candidate Mitt Romney, implied that the president didn't regard the situation gravely enough, wondering out loud how he could appear on the late-night Jay Leno show with the economy in crisis.[19] When the newly inaugurated president translated his salvation narrative into a massive stimulus bill – the $831 billion American Recovery and Reinvestment Act of 2009 – the conservative right, still smarting from its humiliating national defeat, saw an opportunity to go on the attack. They framed the stimulus as deeply anti-democratic. Saul Anuzis, former chair of the Michigan Republican Party, referred to the Obama agenda as "economic fascism."[20] Conservative pundit Michelle Malkin joined South Carolina's governor in denouncing the movement toward a "savior-based economy" ready to bail out entitled and undeserving masses.[21]

When positive economic results from the stimulus were not immediately forthcoming, Obama's promises of heroic transformation began to seem vulnerable, if not empty. Public opinion about the way in which the president was dealing with the economy began a slow but steady downward spiral, and a thoroughgoing pollution of the president's first major legislative victory seemed possible. By August, 2009, six months after its passage, 57 percent of adults thought the stimulus package was "having no impact on the economy or making it worse," and only 18 percent said it had "done anything to help improve their personal situation."[22] While Obama's overall job approval rating held steady in the mid-50s, on the economy it had tanked, falling from 54 percent in September to 46 percent by the beginning of November.[23]

When his promise to heroically transform the economic crisis did not come to pass, the president appeared, to a growing number of Americans, weak and impotent. It seemed there were forces much mightier than he himself. In the first interview of the 2010 New Year, Obama responded to a question about the people who were now feeling "deflated" after feeling so hopeful one year earlier, during the inauguration: "They have every right to feel deflated because the economy was far worse than any of us expected ... People have rightly been anxious this year."[24] President Obama could not transform chaos into order and create a peaceful and abundant world. He had not been able to act as a hero in America's time of need. Just one year after re-election, a *Wall Street Journal*/NBC News survey found the country "in a decidedly negative mood" when it came to the economy.[25] It seemed as if Obama were ready to admit being defeated by events rather than being in control of them: "What I haven't been able to do in the midst of this crisis is bring the country together in a way that we had done in the Inauguration. That's what's been lost this year ... that whole sense of changing how Washington works." It was time to beg the American public for a second chance: "And so this year, refocusing on how – whether we're Democrats or Republicans – we all have common values and care about our kids; we all want work that's satisfying, pays the bills and gives children a better future and security. Returning to those themes is going to be really important."[26]

It didn't work.

Defeat and Disconnection

Liberals who had supported candidate Obama complained that, during his performance as president, he had disappeared from the stage, that he didn't engage in speech-making and made little effort to rally popular support. Actually, President Obama had tried doing all of this. The problem was that his performances failed to reach the hearts and minds of the sharply fragmented audiences he faced. The left was angry and vituperative because the president had abandoned the public option on healthcare and had not nationalized the banks.[27] The center was disappointed because he seemed to have embraced the very big government tools the left accused him of shirking. The right, already embittered at the assumption of power by such a liberal and non-traditional politician, became politically enraged. They began taking over the public stage. In early January, 2010, conservative *New York Times* columnist David Brooks narrated a somber New Year's message about the state of the nation, blaming the "new administration" for not having "galvanized a popular majority:"

> The United States opens this decade in a sour mood. First, Americans are anxious about the future. Sixty-one percent of Americans believe the country is in decline ... Only 27 percent feel confident that their children's generation will be better off than they are. Second, Americans have lost faith in their institutions. During the great moments of social reform, at least 60 percent of Americans trusted government to do the right thing most of the time. Now, only a quarter have that kind of trust. The country is evenly divided about President Obama, but state governments are in disrepute and confidence in Congress is at withering lows ... The Ipsos/McClatchy organizations have been asking voters which party can do the best job of handling a range of 13 different issues. During the first year of the Obama administration, the Republicans gained ground on all 13.[28]

A moment full of foreboding for Obama's presidency came later in January, with the loss of Ted Kennedy's Massachusetts Senate seat to Republican candidate Scott Brown. In the president's telling, nothing less than America's future was on the line. Just 48 hours before the election, he stood at the side of Democratic candidate Martha Coakley and pleaded: "Understand what's at stake here, Massachusetts. It's whether we're going forwards or backwards."[29] Indeed, the election represented an enormous Republican victory. Giving the conservative party a 41st Senate seat, it wiped out the Democrats' super majority and, along with it, seemingly any chance of passing healthcare reform. Hardline conservatives such as Michelle Malkin called it the "Massachusetts miracle."[30] Stunned Democrats lamented the loss, even before the polls had closed. Democratic senator Russ Feingold indicated that it would be "back to the drawing board" on healthcare.[31] Howard Dean suggested an even bigger reversal: "I don't think this was a backlash on health care reform, I think it was a backlash on Washington."[32] Democratic strategist Jerome Armstrong presaged the midterm disaster, tweeting, "This is what Nov 2 will look like unless D's get their act together."[33] Senior advisor David Axelrod admitted, "It was a classic case of everybody getting caught napping."[34] The president, in an interview with television news commentator George Stephanopoulos, reflected on his performative failure: "I think the assumption was if I just focus on policy, if I just focus on this provision or that law or if we're making a good rational decision here, then people will get it."[35]

What people were "getting" instead, apparently, was the counter-narrative projected by the newly energized Tea Party. Candidate Brown had been embraced by the movement, which, through the political action committee (PAC) "Our Country Deserves Better," spent nearly $350,000 on his senatorial campaign.[36] Movement supporters were elated by the victory, which afforded them newfound confidence. "For us, this is not so much about Scott Brown as it is about the idea that if we really collaborate as a mass movement, we can take any seat in the country," exclaimed Eric Odom, executive director of the American Liberty Alliance.[37] *New York Times* editors announced, "The Tea Party movement may be fringe no more,"[38] referring to an NBC News/*Wall Street Journal* survey that found respondents felt less negatively about it (21 percent) than they felt about the Democrats or the Republicans (both at 38 percent).[39] "The movement is maturing," said Judson Phillips, founder of Tea Party Nation, the social networking site that sponsored the inaugural National Tea Party Convention in February.[40]

Rather than acknowledging that the Tea Party was winning the struggle for meaning, Obama's response to the humiliating loss in Massachusetts was to intensify his search for demonstrable legislative achievement. If he could show, in some objective sense, that the political tempest of 2009 had not all been for naught, perhaps Americans would change their minds about who was morally in the right.

Indeed, in April 2010, right after the surprising, if squeaky thin, passage of Obama's healthcare legislation, there was a moment when the sunlight rays of the hero's power seemed briefly to break through the gathering clouds. After that legislative triumph, Obama was headlined and hailed as a "Giant-Killer, Feeling his Oats."[41] "Could Obama Be Invincible?" the *New York Times* asked.[42] Its op-ed columnist Frank Rich headlined: "It's a Bird, It's a Plane, It's Obama."[43] The president happily agreed with these assessments of his transcendent status. Harking back to his earlier promises, in the 2008 campaign, to be the vehicle of dramatic social transformation, he exclaimed: "This is what change looks like . . . Tonight, we answered the call of history."[44]

He *had* done something historic, and it *is* what political change looks like. But in the days after congressional Democrats were able finally to pass the Affordable Care Act, only 32 percent of Americans told pollsters they liked it.[45] Two weeks after its passage, President Obama's job performance ratings slid to 44 percent.[46]

The Deep Water Horizon spill in the Gulf of Mexico, in mid-April, 2010, put an oily tamper on any lingering glory. In the face of British Petroleum's raw, world-transforming power to destroy nature, the president of the United States once again seemed helpless and supine. After 56 days of the oil crisis and counting, Maureen Dowd quipped: "The man who walked on water is now snared by a crisis underwater."[47] Nearly half of Americans polled on June 20 (48 percent) disapproved of the way Obama was handling the oil spill.[48] An influential African American graphic-columnist for the *New York Times*, Charles Blow, announced "the thrill is gone," described the Obama administration as "on the skids," and lamented the "disappointment and sadness lurking just beneath the surface" of the liberal electorate.[49] "Mr. Unpopular," *TIME Magazine* headlined at the end of August.[50] With the 2010 congressional election looming, the *New York Times* warned that "Obama needs to *inspire* Americans" (italics added) and "rally the nation around a big idea."[51] But by then it was too late. The two-year performance of "Obama power" had failed to persuade. Once-receptive audiences were walking away, and they did not return on Election Day.

The American audience was restless and inattentive. Yet, rather than fashioning a new narrative that might have resonated more widely with the American people, the president seemed determine to stick as closely as possible to facts, as if institutional performance could transform itself into compelling cultural story. In the months leading up to the 2010 midterm elections, Obama spoke frequently about his successes to date – healthcare reform, a new credit card law that dealt with hidden fees, financial industry reform, and saving the country "from a Great Depression."[52] He seemed oblivious to the possibility that, when framed within the counter-narrative constructed by his increasingly outspoken conservative opponents, it was these very legislative accomplishments that could seal his political defeat. As a Fox News reporter covering the battleground states put it, the midterm election was "shaping up as a referendum on the [Tea Party] movement's small government message versus President Obama's big government agenda."[53]

In the midst of this gathering political storm, even the most liberal commentators were busy recoding Obama's character. A *New Yorker* journalist observed that even the president's "temperament" had become a political liability: "In 2008, his calm was a synergistic counterpoint to the joyous excitement of the throngs that packed his rallies. In the tidy, quiet isolation of the White House, his serene rationality has felt to many like detachment, even indifference."[54] Obama's character now seemed off-key, and his performance was failing to connect. In the week before the election, a Bloomberg poll found that "some two-thirds of likely voters believed that, under Obama and the Democrats, middle-class taxes have gone up, the economy has shrunk, and the billions lent to banks under the Troubled Asset Relief Program are gone, never to be recovered." None of this was remotely accurate.[55] But empirical facts do not a narrative make. Stories are built upon a simple but compelling dichotomy, one that poses courageous and righteous protagonists against cowardly and evil antagonists. In America's public imagination, President Obama was being gradually shifted to the negative side.

The *New York Times* reported that the Democrats were "playing defense in every corner of the country."[56] The GOP maintained an average 10-point lead among independent voters for much of 2010, and the so-called "enthusiasm gap" measuring the electorate's interest in the race "favored Republicans by an even greater margin."[57] In the pre-election primaries, in what a political analyst for the *Wall Street Journal* called "the battle of the ballots," Republicans seemed to be headed to the polls far more often than Democrats, a once standard trend that had been reversed during the 2002 and 2006 midterm elections.[58] Among Tea Party supporters, who were more likely to classify themselves as "angry,"[59] three quarters were "intensely interested" in the election.[60] As early as April, nearly a quarter of US voters (24 percent) reported that they considered themselves a part of the movement.[61] Unable to counter his growing radio-activity, President Obama suggested that the only way he could help vulnerable Democratic candidates was by distancing himself, by not campaigning for them – by staying away.[62]

In the November, 2010 mid-term elections, Republicans scored an historic victory, taking power in the House of Representatives, where the Tea Party Caucus now numbered in the 80s. Democrats just barely retained control of the Senate. In the immediate wake of this humiliating defeat, the president continued to emphasize instrumental results rather than symbolic action: "The message of the election is I need to do a better job. I need to take direct responsibility for slow progress."[63] Nothing could have been further from the truth. The president had lost control of his transformative narrative. "Americans are not optimistic that he can achieve that goal [of bringing greater civility to politics]," one pollster remarked: "[O]nly a third believe he can end the partisan gridlock in Washington."[64] Obama's poll ratings had tanked. In the mid-50s during the summer of 2009, favorable judgments of his presidency were now sunk in the 40s.[65] The Republicans were in the symbolic driver's seat. It was they who had become the protagonists in America's political play.

Two years later, in November, 2012, the Republicans were pushed to the back of the bus. Restless and inattentive audiences on the left and center had returned to their seats and were enthusiastically applauding the performance of Obama's "last campaign." With an electoral victory over Mitt Romney of 51 to 47 percent, and 332 to 206 in the Electoral College, President Obama became only the second Democrat in 70 years to be re-elected to a second term, the fourth in the past century to receive more than 50 percent of the vote in both presidential elections. He had learned how to inspire Americans while governing them. In the chapters that follow, we describe the re-inflation of Obama's symbolic power and explain what caused it.

3

Re-Inflation

What triggered the change in Obama's political fortunes? It was a new reflection on the relationship between politics and style – on the performative aspects of power. Like a star actor reflecting on a sudden string of bad reviews. Or a producer thinking about how to revive a hit show that has fallen on hard times. It was not the fault of his policies, the president decided. Nor were his Republican opponents to blame. It was not even the news media. The fault was not in the stars but in himself.

In the middle of the Democrats' long downward slide to symbolic deflation, in March 2010, the head of the Obama production team, image-maker-in-chief David Axelrod, had publicly professed to being "baffled" about "why we haven't broken through more than we have." Blaming the "dirty filter" of the media, the famed campaign consultant attacked journalists for their "every day is election day mentality."[1] But this was, in fact, exactly the mentality that President Obama would have to learn. For governing to be successful, every day *must* be Election Day.

In early February, 2009, the newly inaugurated President Obama had described himself as an "eternal optimist," professing to believe that "over time people respond to civility and rational argument."[2] Later that year, speaking at Walter Cronkite's funeral at Lincoln Center in September, he described the legendary anchorman as having earned the title of the "most trusted man in America" because of "his belief that the American people were hungry for the truth, unvarnished and unaccompanied by theater or spectacle."³ After the eruption of the Tea Party, the shocking loss of Senator Teddy Kennedy's long-held Massachusetts Senate seat, and the growing popular resistance to his healthcare legislation, a chastened president was not nearly so complacent, or at least publicly naive. In an interview one year into his presidency, in January 2010, with ABC News' George Stephanopoulos, Obama offered this acknowledgement:

> I was so busy getting stuff done and dealing with immediate crises in front of us, that I think we lost some of that sense of speaking directly to the America people about what their core values are and why we have to make sure those institutions are matching their values."

The president was saying he had lost the feel for his audience. What the American people "ended up seeing," he continued, "is this feeling of remoteness and detachment where, you know, there's these technocrat up here" in Washington.⁴

Fast-forward two and a half years later to July, 2012, and a symbolically re-inflated President Obama sits beside Michelle on the "CBS This Morning" show. Responding to a question from the celebrity interviewer Charlie Rose – about the apparent change in his political fortunes – the president looks back on his learning curve. It is story-telling, not policy, that defines presidential success:

> The mistake of my first term – [first] couple of years – was thinking that this job was just about getting the policy right. And that's important. But the nature of this office is also to tell a story to the American people that gives them a sense of unity and purpose and

optimism, especially during tough times. It's funny – when I ran, everybody said, "Well he can give a good speech but can he actually manage the job?" And in my first two years, I think the notion was, "Well, he's been juggling and managing a lot of stuff, but where's the story that tells us where he's going?" And I think that was a legitimate criticism.[5]

Charlie Rose pressed the president about what it was, exactly, he had to explain better to the American people. The president countered that, yes, he *had* wanted to do more "explaining, *but also inspiring*." Michelle Obama immediately added, "Because hope is still there."[6]

This exchange ricocheted around the nation's newspapers.[7]

If liberal and center audiences did eventually regain hope, it was because President Obama found a way to become a collective symbol of democratic ideals once again.

For that to happen, the timelines of heroic narrative had to be changed. In 2008, candidate Obama had presented himself as a transformative figure, but, in the first two years of President Obama, nothing seem to have changed: the economy was still stuck in the ditch and, despite the giant stimulus and ambitious new banking and health legislation, the everyday lives of ordinary Americans were pretty much the same.

Narratives are culture structures that mark time with beginnings, middles, and ends. If the time of his presidency was economically depressed and politically polarized, the ending of Obama's story had become tragic, his narrative a deflationary movement from hope to despair. In late 2010, Obama and his production team subtly altered this construction of historical time. They reconfigured "now" – contemporary time, his first term in office – as the middle, not the end of the Pilgrim's Progress. The narrative arc of the Barack Obama story was stretched out. The promise would be kept, but "when" was changed. Salvation would still come, just not right now. It would come in the future, later but not much later, sometime toward the end of the president's second term.

In the midst of the 2010 defeat, Michelle Obama spoke at a fundraising event for the Democratic senator Russ Feingold, saying:

> Many of us came into this expecting to see all the change we talked about happen all at once, right away, the minute Barack walked through the Oval Office door ... But the truth is it's going to take longer to dig ourselves out of this hole than any of us would like.[8]

The Democratic majority whip in the House, African American James E. Clyburn of South Carolina, declared "people are beginning to see [that] these expectations" – for Obama to have turned the country around in two years – "would not be out of line if the president were a magician!"[9] Two weeks before the 2010 voting, President Obama sought to assure a youthful crowd: "This is just the start of the journey."[10]

In the wake of the Democrats' 2010 electoral humiliation, the freshly minted symbolic authority of the House Republican majority, and simple arithmetic, made further liberal legislation impossible. Faced with this new reality, President Obama could have retreated from the left to the center and fiddled with moderately conservative forms of legislative compromise. Bill Clinton had done exactly that in the wake of his own legislative Armageddon nearly two decades before.

What Obama did, instead, was to eschew governmental action for speech acts, all the while maintaining his position on the left. Early in 2011, Matt Bai, an inside-the-beltway political reporter for the *New York Times*, reported a "profound shift ... away from legislative priorities to telling a broader American story."[11] Around the same time, in their briefing to reporters before the president's State of the Union Address in January, 2011, senior White House aides used terms like "story" and "painting a picture" to frame expectations.[12] In the address itself, the president proposed a bipartisan effort to "win the future."[13] In its report on the speech, *TIME Magazine* suggested that, "two years into his presidency, Obama has discovered the power of storytelling."[14]

It was during this turn toward story-telling that Gabrielle Giffords, a liberal Arizona congresswoman, was shot in Tucson, Arizona – a ghastly, bloody attempt at political assassination[15] in which six bystanders died. In the aftermath of this event, President Obama was able to place himself at the center of a tragic national drama of mourning and repentance. Seizing the moment in a soaring nationally televised speech before a hushed and reverent Tucson audience, the president called Americans to a new era of civility and demanded that politicians in Washington stop their "point scoring and pettiness."[16] Afterwards, almost seven in ten Americans told pollsters they were deeply impressed by the president's Tucson speech.[17]

Another transfixing event that provided an opportunity to narratively reboot the Obama story occurred several months later, in May 2011, when American Special Forces killed Osama bin Laden. In its immediate aftermath, conservative commentators and some Bush cabinet members tried giving credit to the earlier, Republican president's war-on-terror line. These efforts at cultural reconstruction soon faded, however, as it became evident that Obama had been personally in charge of pre-raid planning and had given the go-ahead order despite the anxieties of his most powerful advisors. If the raid had floundered, as had the Iran hostage rescue during President Jimmy Carter's re-election campaign, the risks to Obama's symbolic authority would have been grave. The background story of what was widely portrayed as Obama's "gutsy" and "patriotic" decision circulated widely, amidst growing national exaltation over the elimination of America's most dangerous foreign antagonist. For the first time in his presidency, Obama played the lead in a macho military play. His approval rating shot up to 57 percent, after stagnating for some time in the mid-40s.[18]

The late night address he made on the day of the Osama murder drew his largest television audience since the election, with about 56.5 million viewers, or about 57 percent of the people watching at that moment.[19] The story he told reached across the boundary of politics into the worlds of religion, family, and military, connecting them all to sacred civil ideals. The speech strung together the sadness and grief of 9/11 – "empty seats at the dinner table" – with the post-attack solidarity of a country "united as one American family" and the "tireless and heroic work" of the military and counter-terrorism professionals. The president concluded by reaffirming that "the United States is not – and never will be – at war with Islam."[20]

The narrative of the fall 2010 elections had pitted an amorphously defined Democratic "government" against a sharply etched Tea Party "movement." Now, Tea Party politicians had taken control of an actual institution, the House of Representatives. And across the Washington Mall they faced, not a vaguely defined government, but Barack Obama. With such easily recognized antagonists and protagonists, the dramatic possibilities for the president enlarged.

President Obama cast himself as lead character in a story about a good willed, democratically elected leader fighting for civil ideals against a recalcitrant, extremist, and bitterly partisan anti-civil other side. Indeed, immediately upon assuming power, House conservatives began squabbling among themselves, united only by their unrelenting opposition to virtually every action undertaken by the Democratic president. The infighting led an influential Republican political advisor to remark on how challenging it was to find "reasonable rational voices" among House Republicans, instead of "boisterous conservatives" who looked "kooky" to the American people.[21] He was questioning the civil character of his own side. For his part,

President Obama was beginning to have some success at pre-senting himself as a public figure working at "finding common ground," in marked contrast with the polarizing character he had been made out to be in the two first years of his term. Three out of four Americans now identified the president in this manner, less than half attributing to the Republican Congress equally civil intentions.[22]

Building on this symbolic re-inflation, Obama began to reconstruct the "performance" of his power. For the first time in his presidency, he persuasively presented himself as speaking on behalf of all the people, or at least for those citizens who were not too violent, too right wing, or too rich. He entered into this more sacred position in American political culture by focusing on the seemingly mundane issue of the budget.

The Republican House had declared deficit reduction its number one priority. The president announced he would with-hold his own proposals until the House showed its hand. The Republicans finally passed the so-called "Ryan Budget" in April 2011,[23] proposing to transform Medicare, the universal system for older Americans, into a private sector voucher system, and to slash Medicaid for the poor, all the while maintaining Bush-era tax cuts for the wealthiest Americans. It was at this point that the Democratic protagonist in the White House pounced. He would not allow the budget to be balanced on the "backs of people who are poor or people who are powerless or don't have lobbyists or don't have clout,"[24] merely to enable the wealthiest Americans, who had already benefited from decades of conserv-ative tax indulgences, to continue to receive tax relief. Putting forth his own budget proposal, the president asserted: "It's an approach that puts every kind of spending on the table – but one that protects the middle class, our promise to seniors, and our investments in the future."[25] Obama insisted that tax rates on the rich must be raised, supplying revenue that would move the budget toward balance without cutting services for those who needed them the most. It was time for wealthy Americans to demonstrate the commitment to a more expansive, more civil kind of solidarity:

I say that at a time when the tax burden on the wealthy is at its lowest level in half a century, the most fortunate among us can afford to pay a little more. I don't need another tax cut. Warren Buffett doesn't need another tax cut. Not if we have to pay for it by making seniors pay more for Medicare. Or by cutting kids from Head Start. Or by taking away college scholarships that I wouldn't be here without. That some of you wouldn't be here without. And I believe that most wealthy Americans would agree with me. They want to give back to the country that's done so much for them. Washington just hasn't asked them to.[26]

Taking it a step further, the president called for eschewing partisanship for the sake of national solidarity: "This sense of responsibility – to each other and to our country – this isn't a partisan feeling. It isn't a Democratic or Republican idea. It's patriotism."[27] The president told supporters in Chicago the following day that the nation stood at a defining moment: "The speech I gave yesterday was not a partisan shot at the other side. It was an attempt to clarify the choice we have as a country right now."[28]

The president made these proposals about government taxing and spending in what he would later characterize as his own, "grow from the middle out" budget, and it was on this basis that he sought to negotiate a "grand bargain" with House leader Boehner.[29]

The left was overjoyed at what they saw as a progressive move by the president. Obama's landmark speech announcing the budget was, in the words of one opinion editor at the *Washington Post*, "the most ambitious defense he may have ever attempted of American liberalism and of what it means to be a Democrat."[30] "It was very nice to see the president channel some of the anger that not just the progressive base is feeling, but that I think the whole country is feeling," intoned Ilyse Hogue, the former political director at MoveOn.[31] Not surprisingly, from the right, the *Wall Street Journal* called the speech "toxic," accusing the president of "blistering partisanship."[32] Congressman Ryan's response was no less unkind: "I'm very disappointed in the president . . . Rather than building bridges, he's poisoning wells."[33]

When, as expected, the Tea Party Republicans in control of the House refused to budge, the president set out on a barnstorming, campaign-style tour around the United States, during which, according to the liberal critic Robert Reich, he had "rediscovered his voice."[34] Promoting a budget that translated social solidarity into deficit-balancing tax reform, and which promised to chip away at economic inequality at the same time, the president dramatically evoked the "vision of America in which we are connected to one another, [where] I am my brother's keeper, I am my sister's keeper."[35] The man who had designed the Republican's spending-slashing, low tax maintaining budget, Representative Ryan, went on a campaign tour of his own – throughout his Wisconsin district. But while drawing much praise, he was booed and heckled by some of his angry audiences, as were some of the other Republican members of Congress who presented the bill to their constituents.[36] Clearly, the budget debate had turned into a mortal political battle, the *New York Times* citing a former Republican staff director of the Senate Budget Committee: "[It] is the big one, and goes to the very major questions about the role of government. This is going to be a very fundamental clash of ideologies."[37] Media on both sides of the ideological aisle invoked metaphors such as "battle," "fight," "attack," and "war."[38] The *Wall Street Journal's* Daniel Henninger declared Obama's fiscal policy speech "an invitation to the Gunfight at the OK Corral."[39]

The dramatic stakes were high indeed, and the denouement was telling. In the months-long face-off that ensued, 72 percent of Americans blamed Republicans, not the Democratic president, for the breakdown of negotiations.[40] Negative views of the Tea Party began to rise. Back on Election Day 2010, four in ten voters had declared themselves Tea Party supporters. Nine months later, in the late summer of 2011, only 20 percent of Americans said they agreed with Tea Party positions, and four out of ten now declared themselves resolutely opposed.[41] In November, the Pew Research Center reported that even conservative strongholds were wavering. During the 2010 election period, "agreement with the Tea Party far outweighed disagreement in the 60 House districts represented by members of the Congressional Tea Party Caucus," and only 10 percent disagreed with the party; a year later this sentiment sharply rose to 23 percent.[42] As this evidence on audience reception suggests, the president's new narrative had resonance. Members of the center were reconnecting with Obama, distancing themselves from the framing offered by the Republican side. The leading characters in the nation's political drama had switched sides. Ultra-conservative Republicans, once heroic rebels, were increasingly viewed as antagonists, and, for the first time since the beginning of his presidency, Obama was being seen as the good guy.[43]

The president announced he was giving up any hope of reaching agreement with what he characterized as a stubborn, bitterly partisan, privilege-defending Republican majority. "I am not going to have a one-sided deal that hurts the folks most vulnerable," he explained.[44] He declared that he would let the American people decide who was right, that the direction of the country would be decided by the presidential election looming on the political horizon, now just one year away.

Even as Obama faced some of his lowest presidential approval ratings, in the summer and fall of 2011,[45] his new hero narrative was steadily amassing symbolic credit, as the sharp decline in Tea Party support dramatically demonstrated. The public opinion data on the success of his presidency were unsurprising in light of the still tepid condition of the economy, but their larger effect – on his personal poll ratings and, ultimately, on the possibility of his re-election – were mitigated in significant ways. And even though "a slight majority of Americans for the first time blamed President Obama either a great deal (24%) or a moderate amount (29%) for the nation's economic problems," they still were much more likely to blame Bush: "Nearly 7 in 10 blame Bush a great deal (36%) or a moderate amount (33%)."[46] There had been an early surge in the president's approval ratings as he prepared for his State of the Union address in early 2011 – up 8 percent from December, according to a poll taken after the shooting of Gabrielle Giffords. Finally, according to a *Wall Street Journal*/NBC poll, "among political independents, positive views of Mr. Obama's job performance surpassed negative views for the first time since August 2009."[47]

But the unemployment rate held firm in the months that followed, wavering between 8.9 and 9.1 percent,[48] and job growth remained relatively stagnant.[49] The substantial number of people who had earlier reported confidence that the economy would improve in 2011 (40 percent[50]) were sorely disappointed by the end of the summer, when more than 70 percent of Americans thought the economy hadn't yet hit rock-bottom.[51] As one of America's leading political statisticians[52] Nate Silver reminded liberals, on his *FiveThirtyEight* blog for the *New York Times*, such poor economic numbers could result in "something of a feedback loop, with diminishing confidence in Mr. Obama, diminishing confidence in the economy, and an actual decline in economic performance all reinforcing one another."[53]

What the president had laid against this possibility was his growing symbolic dominance over conservatives, from the Tea Party to Congress. As the 112th Congress had convened in

January 2011, the public felt more or less equally confident about the abilities of the Republican legislators and the president to "handle the major issues facing the country."[54] But as the budget battle became protracted and Obama moved toward narrative domination, public opinion of Congress plummeted, dropping 10 points and reaching an astounding low of 9 percent by the fall.[55] Obama's job performance rating, meanwhile, held steady, ranging between 43 and 47 percent,[56] even as a significant majority of Americans was dissatisfied with the condition of the country.[57] When the debt ceiling negotiations reached a crescendo over the summer, just 21 percent approved of the way Congress was handling them, while more than twice that number approved of the president's actions (46 percent).[58] In mid-September, the grim reportage by the *New York Times* summed up how the country felt about Congress:

> Only 6 percent of registered voters say that most members of Congress have earned re-election, while 84 percent say it's time to give someone new a chance, a historic low for the *New York Times/CBS* poll. Dissatisfaction with Congress runs deep across both parties, with more than 8 in 10 of both Republicans and Democrats saying it's time to elect new representatives.[59]

The contrasting steadiness of Obama's job performance ratings was sustaining his symbolic capacity for narrative recovery. So were his personal ratings, which did more than hold steady. A September 2011 poll taken by the *Wall Street Journal/*NBC showed that 70 percent of Americans liked the president personally, whether they approved of his policies or not.[60] The audience of citizens was receptive to Obama assuming the protagonist position in America's quickening political play.

4

Setting the Stage

In autumn of 2011, the newly energized story-telling president took off his gloves. Having given up compromising, he turned his ploughshare into a sword and entered full, partisan campaign mode. The presidential protagonist was now symbolizing on all four cylinders, presenting himself as a hero defending the nation against the Republican effort to destroy social solidarity. A large part of this forward-moving narrative referenced the economy. At a fundraiser at a private home in Washington, DC, the president spoke about how his administration had prevented a "total economic meltdown":

> We were able to prevent America from going into a Great Depression ... We were able to, after a series of quarterly GDP reports that were the worst that we've seen since the Great Depression, reverse it and get the economy to grow again. We've seen 20 straight months of consecutive job growth.

But he humbly acknowledged the hero's job was yet unfinished: "A lot of people are still struggling out there. And there's no way in which America right now is fulfilling all of its potential."[1]

At this very moment, the field of Republican presidential contenders was coming into view, the immensely wealthy former Massachusetts governor Mitt Romney apparently

securely in the lead.[2] For the Obama production team, Romney
was a figure sent from central casting, suited perfectly to play
either the fool or the dark knight in the unfolding presidential re-election script. In November, 2011, the *Times* reported
that "Mr. Obama's aides were highly focused on Mr. Romney
almost from the moment the Republican field took shape this
summer."[3] The Democratic National Committee (DNC) took
aim at Romney immediately. Democratic allies produced an
ad in early November entitled, "Mitt Romney's America," portraying what the country would look like if the frontrunner
for the Republican nomination actually became president: Wall
Street "unregulated," Main Street "isolated," the middle-class
"decimated," and American jobs "relocated," among other terrifying prospects.[4] Later that month, "Mitt v. Mitt" portrayed
the Republican contender as a flip-flopper.[5]

Coming months before the actual beginning of the re-
election campaign, this aggressive symbolic work was widely
noticed and intensely discussed. Traditionally, campaign treas-
uries had saved their media money for the home stretch. The
Obama production team was radically changing the sequence
of symbolic representation. They publicly acknowledged their
ambition; it was to "define" Romney in the public imagination long before he would have the opportunity, as the party's
nominee, to define himself. Democratic officials explained that
Obama campaign leaders "want to move early to undermine
the image he [Romney] is trying to build as a can-do businessman,"[6] and campaign advisors "made clear that they would
cast him [Romney] as out of touch with the concerns of middle-
class Americans."[7] Symbolic domination is demonstrated when
one performer begins to write his opponent's script.

Just as Obama was finding the sweet spot of social solidarity,
defending the "middle class" of ordinary men and women, in
walked a figure from stage right, a man who, even by his own
accounts, fairly shouted out "economic interests" and "free

markets." Romney was playing a back-to-the-future character. An extraordinary success in private life, the public Romney presented himself as a kind of anti-icon; in fact, his production team had chosen to make the formerly moderate Massachusetts governor even more "exquisitely one-dimensional: The All-Businessman, the world's most boring superhero."[8] The aim of Team Obama was to code this emphasis on business and free markets as dangerously undermining the social solidarity upon which democracy depends.

As a willing and able symbol of the business mentality, this Romney-character made remarks such as "I like being able to fire people,"[9] "corporations are people, my friend,"[10] and "I'm not concerned about the very poor."[11] He withheld information about the extent and nature of his wealth, refusing to release more than one year's tax returns[12] or to disclose how much of his wealth was parked in tax-avoidances off-shore.[13] While all this was perfectly legal, and even made sense from a competitively economic point of view, it was matter out of place in the civil sphere. To many observers, the wealthy Republican contender seemed secretive, even furtive, far from the ideals of openness and transparency that democratic politics demands. Romney was having visible difficulty shifting from the openly selfish struggle for economic wealth to the earnestly altruistic contest for democratic political power. The *Wall Street Journal* began to worry about what it called Romney's "likeability deficit."[14]

Indeed, Romney was not nearly as well liked as Obama.[15] He suffered from what columnist Jonah Goldberg aptly described in an op-ed for the *Los Angeles Times* as "an authentic inauthenticity problem," with Goldberg going on to flatly call him "politically fake."[16] While at this early point the presumptive Republican and Democratic contenders were polling as equally matched in a hypothetical presidential race, with Romney viewed better suited to handle the economy's problems, the

Republican already suffered from a serious symbolic disadvantage. Liberals condemned him for moving away from being a moderately liberal governor in Massachusetts, for what they saw as kowtowing to the religious right and to those who were anti-feminist, anti-gay, anti-immigrant, and super-rich. Conservatives didn't like him; despite his reassurances that he had changed, they didn't trust him as "one of us." The center did not hold either, distrusting Romney for his lack of moderation or for changing his mind. The first polls of the 2012 New Year showed a stark gap in ways Americans felt about the two men. In terms of "basic feelings," Obama led Romney 42 percent to 28 percent. And the gap grew wider when respondents were asked whether they liked the man; 66 percent liked Obama, compared with just 44 percent for Romney.[17] When it came to "cares about people like me," 51 percent thought this described Obama "somewhat" or "very" well, compared to 41 percent for Romney, a gap that widened for "cares about the poor" (64 vs. 38 percent). Conversely, with "cares about the wealthy," Romney far outpaced Obama, 89 to 55 percent.[18] According to you.gov.com, "the data get worse for Romney" when citizens considered his personal wealth:

> The better one thinks "personally wealthy" describes Romney, the better one thinks that "cares about the wealthy" describes him (the correlation is 0.60). But the same correlation for Obama is much smaller (0.18). People's perception that Obama is personally wealthy does not translate as strongly into the perception that he cares about the wealthy.[19]

Just as Obama began, in autumn 2011, to frame Romney as the very embodiment of anti-solidarity, the Occupy Wall Street movement erupted on America's public stage. In traditional political terms, the left-wing protest accomplished little, and, as an organization, it soon disappeared from the American scene. Culturally, however, the radical performance of protest achieved a great deal more. It crystallized rhetoric about what had, until then, largely been an academic discussion about growing economic inequality. Attacking the 1 percent on behalf of the other 99, Occupy was a tipping point, opening the gates for more full-throated demands for equality in the mainstream. The president, the *Times* reported in early December, 2011, was now "infusing his speech with the moralistic language that has emerged in the Occupy protests around the nation."[20] His senior advisor, David Plouffe, made it known that the production team intended to make Wall Street reform "one of the central elements of the campaign next year."[21]

The president had seized upon populist language that began to resonate with most Americans. In a *Wall Street Journal*/NBC poll, three-quarters of the country agreed with the statement:

> The current economic structure of the country is out of balance and favors a very small proportion of the rich over the rest of the country. America needs to reduce the power of major banks and corporations and demand greater accountability and transparency. The government should not provide financial aid to corporations and should not provide tax breaks to the rich.[22]

It was precisely these concerns that Obama addressed in a major speech given in Osawatomie, Kansas, that formally kicked off his election campaign: "It is wrong. It's wrong that in the United States of America, a teacher or a nurse or a construction worker, [who] maybe earns $50,000 a year, should pay a higher tax rate than somebody raking in $50 million." Obama was aligning himself, via both his rhetoric and in his geographical position, with the iconic Republican Teddy Roosevelt who had been president early in the last century. In 1910, that famously progressive politician had spoken in the same little town, issuing a clarion call for fairness and the right to succeed. "Our country," Roosevelt had proclaimed, "means nothing unless it means the triumph of a real democracy ... of an economic system under which each man shall be guaranteed the opportunity to show the best that there is in him." Obama made this mythically crystallized sentiment his own, bringing it forward as a quintessentially American value for today: "I believe that this country succeeds when everyone gets a fair shot, when everyone does their fair share, when everyone plays by the same rules. These aren't Democratic values or Republican values. These aren't 1 percent values or 99 percent values. They're American values. And we have to reclaim them."[23] Seven months later, David Axelrod would echo this representation: "The viability of the middle class is not a class issue. It's an American issue."[24]

Facing this narrative crescendo, Obama's soon-to-be opponent felt compelled to acknowledge some of its central elements, even while laying claim to a sharply different political opportunity.[25] He denounced the Occupy protests as "dangerous" and "class warfare"[26] – as themselves threatening social solidarity. Then, he seized upon the Occupy movement as a chance to showcase Obama's failures, launching what would become a sustained assault on how the president had handled the economy. Fielding a question about the Occupy movement in New Hampshire in late October, the Republican suggested that some protestors were probably "angry" at being out of work: "So if we had a president who had understood what it took to reboot the American economy and get us back to work, we wouldn't have this problem, or we wouldn't have people protesting, because they'd be working."[27] Eventually, even Romney's own plans for the economy became laced with Occupy rhetoric. At a campaign stop in Arizona in February, 2012, he proposed 20 percent across-the-board tax cuts, to be paid for by limiting deductions and exemptions for "high income folks": "[W]e are going to cut back on that, so we make sure the top one percent pay their fair share or more."[28] Not for the last time, the Republican candidate was playing into the president's hand.

In mid-November, a key Democratic consultant told journalists Romney was a "plutocrat whose brand of capitalism would hurt the interests of the middle class at a moment when the country is increasingly focused on income inequality."[29] By the end of 2011, Obama was traveling the country denouncing the "you're-on-your-own economics" touted by Mitt Romney and his Republican party. It "flies in the face of everything we stand for," the president lamented, planting his feet in the middle of the progressive narrative about inequality undermining the solidarity upon which democracy depends.[30]

The president and his production team now began a months-long construction of the Republican frontrunner as a "Bain-capitalist," not only rhetorically but materially connecting him with the prototypically aggressive 1980s and 1990s investment company. Romney had been the first president and then the CEO of Bain, positions that had earned him such great wealth. Just days before the Iowa caucuses, in early January, 2012, the Obama team moved onto the scene, with "operatives descend[ing] on Iowa to set up an anti-Romney war room at a hotel in downtown Des Moines."[31] They then held a press conference featuring Randy Johnson, a former factory worker at a company Bain Capital had purchased and subsequently closed, laying off about 200 people. According to reports in the *Boston Globe*, the transaction had yielded about $100 million for Bain on its original $5 million investment.[32] Johnson painted a portrait of Romney that perfectly dovetailed with the Democrats' construction of him, saying, "I think he's out of touch with the average person" and "I really think he didn't care about the workers."[33]

As the anti-Bain campaign was unfolding, a shift in the overall economic picture seemed to provide material validation of Obama's year of narrative success. After being stuck at 9 percent for much of 2011, the unemployment rate had fallen to 8.3 by January, 2012,[34] and the drop was more pronounced in a group of states that were anticipated to be hotly contested in the presidential election.[35] The president's job approval rating moved out of its nadir in fall 2011, rising back into the mid-40s, inching closer to the magical level of 50 percent.[36] In what the *Wall Street Journal* called a "sentimental turn," consumer confidence rose sharply over the same period, 10 points from December, 2011, through February, 2012, and a full 20 points since the summer of 2011.[37] The material realm was evolving in a manner that seemed to support Obama's successful shift in the symbolic realm.[38]

During the Republican primary contests that unfolded in the winter months of 2012, Romney's principal opponents built on the Democrat's evident symbolic success. Eagerly jumping on the anti-Bain bandwagon and exploiting what *Politico* called the "Bain Bomb,"[39] they gained some short-lived political traction against the frontrunner. A PAC supporting former Republican House speaker Newt Gingrich released a half-hour documentary that promised a "story of greed"[40] about Romney's tenure at Bain, and Texas governor Rick Perry declared Romney a "vulture capitalist."[41] In the long run, these tactics backfired for the Republican side. They helped separate the stigmatizing construction of Romney from purely partisan motivation, allowing the symbolization of him as anti-civil, secretive, and egotistical to seem more like empirical fact.

Romney and his team pushed back, continuing their onslaught of anti-Obama attacks. Acknowledging that Obama retained some cultural power, and perhaps was even beginning to symbolically re-inflate, Romney deftly carved a wedge between two different, temporally separated "Obamas" – the very personae that the post-2010 president was busy trying to sew back together again. On the one side, there was the

sacred hero elected in 2008, on the other the supposedly
banal failure of the present day: "Three years ago, we measured Candidate Obama by his hopeful promises and slogans.
Today, President Obama has amassed an actual record of debt,
decline and disappointment."[42] Romney also worked to position himself on the sacred side of America's political morality, describing the president's vision as an "entitlement society"
that contrasted with his own promise to create an "opportunity
society." "President Obama wants to fundamentally transform
America," Mr. Romney declared. "He wants to turn America
into a European-style social welfare state. We want to ensure
that we remain a free and prosperous land of opportunity ...
This president takes his inspiration from the capitals of Europe;
we look to the cities and small towns of America."[43] Romney
ratcheted up the significance of the choice, describing the next
election as an historic moment that would determine the possibility of national salvation: "This election is about more than
just replacing the president. It's an election to save the soul of
America."[44] Opportunity over Entitlement = Salvation. The failures of the Democratic president had thrown the country onto
the hinge of history. The nation's soul was endangered. Only the
election of the Republican could save the day.

In the year since his party's humiliating 2010 defeat, President
Obama had regained his sense of narrative and his feel for
the audience. He had successfully painted the new Republican
Congress as a stubborn, mean-spirited, broadly anti-civil
enemy. As he turned from painting Congress to performing his
presidential campaign, Obama's ambition was to extend the
soiled identity of the Republican Congress to the Republican
candidate he would face the following year at election time. But
the contagion would not (yet) spread. Polls in January, 2012,
showed that, when voters thought ahead to the November presidential election, they had not yet put Obama decisively in first
place.[45] The audience sitting at the center of the political theater

would wait to make their choice.[46] For the deal to be closed, the Democratic construction of Romney as anti-civil would have to deepen, the analogical connection between the Republican Party's presidential candidate and the Republicans' polluted Congress more strongly made.

During the Republican nomination fight, Romney's opponents had painted him as a conservative-come-lately, noting how the once moderate Massachusetts governor was running away from his earlier positions, while denying he was doing so every step of the way. With the nomination still undecided, Eric Fehrnstrom, "Mitt Romney's David Axelrod" and the "keeper of the candidate's narrative," made an unfortunate quip that seemed to underscore these very problems in the Romney character.[47] Asked if Romney would be able to move from right-wing fighter for the nomination to centrist campaigner in the general election, Fehrnstrom explained to CNN, "Well, I think you hit a reset button for the fall campaign." He continued: "Everything changes. It's almost like an Etch A Sketch. You can kind of shake it up and we start all over again."[48] Immediately, Republican rivals and Democrats alike pounced, seizing on what the *New York Times* called "the all-too-obvious metaphors: Mr. Romney erasing his positions; 'Mitt 5.0'; Mr. Romney 'reinventing' himself."[49] The *Times* reported that "the Democratic National Committee sent out snarky e-mails hourly" and that "Newt Gingrich and Rick Santorum even trotted out the [Etch A Sketch] toy at campaign rallies."[50] The media, not surprisingly, jumped on the gaffe, critically examining just how variable Romney's positioning had indeed been. According to Nate Silver, "the comments made by the adviser, Eric Fehrnstrom, will serve to remind voters of a major issue in the campaign: that Mr. Romney has substantially altered his positions on a wide range of issues since he ran for governor in Massachusetts in 2002."[51] *Red State*'s Daniel Horowitz quipped, "We have finally discovered our symbol that exemplifies Romney," noting,

"Fehrnstrom's comments have struck such a cord [sic] with the base because they sum up Romney's history in one image. Whenever he needs to win a particular political office, he resets the slate and pollinates it with whatever positions he ascertains to be politically expedient."[52]

As the winter months ticked away, the Obama campaign began to deploy a double-barreled strategy, portraying the wealthy Republican not only as a one-percenter whose privilege threatened solidarity, but as a flip-flopper whose statements on the issues could simply not be trusted. By late April, 2012, after Romney clinched the Republican nomination, the two strategies became one. Obama's smoothly running production team was slightly shifting gears, the *New York Times* reported: "Senior administration officials, along with Democratic and campaign officials, all say their strategy now will be to tell the world that Mr. Romney has a core after all – and it's deep red."[53]

5

Unfolding the Drama

After Romney gained the nomination, in the spring of 2012, the head-to-head, gladiator battle crystallized, the polluting rhetoric about flip-flopping intensified, and the narratives about attacking privilege and restoring a wider, civil solidarity became more elevated and intense. "This is the defining issue of our time," President Obama already declared in April.[1] "This is a make or break moment for the middle class," he cried out in May.[2] It seemed the only thing the president agreed with Romney about was that, in 2012, America was once again balancing on the hinge of history. If a narrative about "the crisis of our times" is established, it can be the making of a hero, if he is up to the job. A dramatic documentary-like campaign promo directed by Academy Award-winner Davis Guggenheim spun silken strings of myth from the Great Depression, and the president who had resolved it, to the Great Recession and the president who was meeting it head on today: "Not since the days of Franklin Roosevelt had so much fallen on the shoulders of one president."[3] At stake was nothing less, that contemporary Democratic president now declared, than whether the nation would move forward into a better future or backward into a dangerously anti-democratic past: "Somehow, [Mr. Romney] and his friends in Congress think that the same bad ideas [as those which guided the Bush years] will lead to a different result . . . [W]e were there. We remember. And we're not going back. We are moving this country forward."[4]

Romney placed the nation on the hinge of history in a sharply contrasting way. He, too, sought to frame contemporary economic troubles as a threat to democracy, but he connected this threat to Obama's moral incapacity. It was not only that there was high unemployment, thanks to Obama's ignorance of business, but that his faltering efforts to address it threatened the sacred moral core of American democracy: "In fact, things are so dire under Obama's 'change' presidency, we are only inches away from no longer being a free economy."[5] On June 1, the latest economic figures were released, showing the lowest level of job creation in a year and the employment rate inching up from 8.1 to 8.2 percent. Romney pounced. Calling the report "devastating news for the American workers and American families," he mocked the president's campaign slogan "forward."[6] Republican John Boehner joined in. Only Romney would allow the country to change: "It's clear that the policies that we have seen are not working . . . It's time for us to change course and have real policies that will put Americans back to work."[7]

The Obama campaign fired back, spending $10 million to release an ad that put Romney far back into the past. In "Heard it Before," the narrator intones, "When Mitt Romney was governor, Massachusetts lost 40,000 manufacturing jobs . . . and fell to forty-seventh in job creation, fourth from the bottom." The ad closes with a dire warning about the future: "Romney economics. It didn't work then and it won't work now."[8] The future was at stake. The only way forward was Obama.

At this point, the Romney character faltered. Defending the austerity policy of balancing the budget through government cuts – the "Ryan Budget" promoted by House conservatives – Romney made a remark that was widely construed as attacking some of America's most mythical occupations: "He [Obama] says we need more firemen, more policemen, more teachers. Did he not get the message of Wisconsin? The American people did. It's time for us to cut back on government and help the American people."[9] The comment seemed to reinforce the Democrats' portrayal of Romney as removed from the everyday reality of most Americans. As New York senator Charles Schumer put it, "Middle-class voters already distrust Mitt Romney for being out-of-touch and uncaring about regular folks. Bragging about wanting to give pink slips to first responders only cements that perception."[10]

Describing Obama as "decider-in-chief," the Democratic campaign took the opportunity of the anniversary of Osama bin Laden's death to paint the presumptive Republican candidate as not brave enough to have made the same decision. A campaign video narrated by former president Bill Clinton quotes Mitt Romney in 2007: "It's not worth moving heaven and earth spending billions of dollars just trying to catch one person."[11] Vice-President Biden offered what he called a new "bumper sticker" message, quipping, "It's pretty simple: Osama bin Laden is dead and General Motors is still alive."[12] The president was presenting himself as a hero, able to save both nation and economy. But the strategy had the potential for backlash. A few current and former navy SEALs expressed distaste, with Ryan Zinke, now a Republican senator in Montana, saying, "I think every president would have done the same … The President and his administration are positioning him as a war president and using the SEALs as ammunition. It was predictable."[13] Even the liberal blogger Adriana Huffington called turning the event into a campaign ad "one of the most despicable things you can do."[14] Nevertheless, the Obama as hero narrative was already long in play. Reminding the American people that he had made the gutsy call to kill public enemy number one was in character.

In late June, 2012, the Supreme Court handed down its verdict on a controversial 2010 Arizona immigration law, which had made it a state crime for undocumented immigrants to fail to carry proper government identification. The court's split decision struck that provision down, and it came right on the heels of a widely publicized Obama administration action offering reprieve from deportation to young immigrants. Hailing the court's decision, the president spoke up for the expansion of a broadly civil rather than a narrow, more primordial solidarity: "What makes us American is not a question of what we look like or what our names are. What makes us American is our shared belief in the enduring promise of this country – and our shared responsibility to leave it more generous and more hopeful than we found it."[15] Once again, Romney seemed able to offer little in response. During the primary campaign, Romney had promoted a markedly less expansive vision of the civil sphere. Defending the traditional American core group against immigrant newcomers, he had bragged to Republican voters that, if elected, his policies would be so harsh that undocumented immigrants would want to "self-deport."[16] Faced with the Supreme Court's more expansive ruling, Romney's default position was to strike at an unfulfilled campaign promise: "As Candidate Obama, he promised to present an immigration plan during his first year in office. But 4 years later, we are still waiting."[17]

One of the early summer's most heated exchanges involved the connection between domestic politics and what happened outside the borders of the US. Not surprisingly, the troubled American economy once again provided the scene. The trigger was a *Washington Post* exposé about Bain Capital and its investments in firms that shipped jobs overseas to China and India. The *New York Times* described how Democrats built on the news to deepen their painting of Romney as elitist and anti-democratic: "Mr. Obama – and a team of campaign aides, operatives and surrogates – took to the airwaves, microphones and the Internet to call his rival out of touch."[18] A television ad created to run in the battleground state of Virginia asked, "Does Virginia really want an outsourcer-in-chief in the White House?"[19] The Romney campaign responded in a narrowly technical manner, distinguishing off-shore investments of capital, which they portrayed as economically productive, from outsourcing jobs. At a campaign event in New Hampshire, the president laughingly derided the Republicans' attempt at nuance: "If you're a worker whose job went overseas, you really don't need somebody explaining you the difference between outsourcing and offshoring."[20]

A spokesperson for Romney offered the following retort: "If President Obama had even half of Mitt Romney's record on jobs, he'd be running on it. But President Obama has the worst record on jobs and the economy of any president in modern history, which is why he is running a campaign based on distractions, not solutions."[21] Obama was a bad economic manager because he did not have the experience of a businessperson, and he was a liar besides.

Punch and counter-punch continued into the summer, each candidate painting the other as dishonest and implicitly connecting this anti-democratic quality to an inability to cure the nation's economic woes. A Romney ad chastised the president for being misleading about the Republican's record, suggesting a pattern of deceit that went back a long way:

> When a president doesn't tell the truth, how can we trust him to lead? The Obama outsourcing attacks: misleading, unfair and untrue. There was no evidence that Mitt Romney shipped jobs overseas. Candidate Obama lied about Hillary Clinton. [voiceover by Hillary Clinton] "So shame on you, Barack Obama." But America expects more from a president. Obama's dishonest campaign: another reason America has lost confidence in Barack Obama.[22]

When the Obama campaign responded with "Romney's big Bain lie," Romney took it to the next level, demanding an apology for what he called "reckless" and "absurd" allegations.[23] The media joined the conversation, the *Wall Street Journal* and the *New York Times* featuring pieces dissecting the veracity of each side's claims.[24] FactCheck.org, a non-partisan group, reported that its investigation of the outsourcing attacks "found no evidence to support the claim that Romney – while he was still running Bain Capital – shipped American jobs overseas."[25] But the Democrats claimed that, even after Romney had stepped down from the Bain presidency, he had remained actively in control as CEO. MarketWatch's Rex Nutting, who checked the facts "behind financial and economic pronouncements of executives, pundits and politicians," tried stepping back from moral incrimination into the neutral zone of fact: "Both parties have good arguments that their opponent has helped outsource jobs, but both sides have also exaggerated their evidence in a way that misleads voters."[26] The *Wall Street Journal* bewailed the pollution and mud-slinging of political strife. Refraining from calling one's opponent a liar should be "one of the unspoken rules of combat."[27]

With four months to go until the election, many national level polls still put the candidates in a statistical dead heat, but Obama's symbolic construction of Romney as an anti-democratic elitist continued to gain resonance.[28] Polls measuring the likeability of the two candidates and their relationship to the American people bore out this damaging anti-civil vision of Romney, attesting to Obama's ability to symbolize social solidarity. Already in May, 2012, Gallup found that registered voters were twice as likely to say Obama was more "likeable." And the gap was larger among independent voters (59 vs. 28 percent). Obama also scored high on "cares about people like you" – 51 vs. 41 percent overall and 53 vs. 37 percent among independents.[29] The only dimension where Romney led

Obama, and only very narrowly, was "can manage the government effectively" – 46 vs. 43 percent overall and 46 vs. 40 among Independents.[30] By the end of June, Romney had gained some points on likeability but Obama still outpaced him 81 to 64 percent. Perhaps even more importantly, the poll measured Obama in the lead on a crucial dimension of civil morality, with 60 percent believing him "honest and trustworthy" as compared to 50 percent for Romney. On a more personal measure of solidarity – "understands the problems Americans face in their daily lives" – Obama again took the lead, 58 vs. 46 percent.[31] Such subjective feelings of connection are highly significant. As *FiveThirtyEight*'s John Sides put it: "Presidential elections are rarely won and lost on policy. Voters instead tend to choose the person they most want to be president based on who they like. And that feeling is heavily influenced by which of the candidates they believe best understands their hopes and dreams."[32]

Romney hoped to continue hammering Obama's economic record by pointing to objective facts, such as the relatively high unemployment rate and the lack of significant job creation.[33] Obama's team contextualized these facts by linking them to pure and polluted moral categories. "If Mitt Romney wins, the middle class loses,"[34] the president proclaimed in late June. He portrayed Romney as using "every trick in the book" to avoid his fair share of taxes, accusing him of violating the sacred of the civil code of honesty: "What is Mitt Romney hiding?"[35]

Meaning is all about contrast, and establishing difference became the name of the game. According to the Wesleyan Media Project, by May a total of 70 percent of campaign ads had been negative, as compared to just 9 percent at the same point in the 2008 election.[36] By November, this number would be 79 percent for Romney and 86 percent for Obama.[37] Potential voters in swing states were inundated with portrayals of Obama as lacking the competence to do anything about the economy and of Romney as a symbol for why the economy went bad to begin with. It was a battle between two candidates, each of whom represented himself as an economic savior. Romney's default position was a set of terrifying statistics: "40 straight months of unemployment over eight percent" and "23 million Americans can't find jobs." As if these data were not scary enough, the Republican weighted them with gender morality: "Under Obama, 800,000 more women are unemployed."[38]

The president was intent on separating his opponent from the narrative of forward progress that a hero needs to sustain: "Mitt Romney's not the solution. He's the problem."[39]

While Romney had little difficulty putting points on the board, he had problems narrating himself heroically, a necessary cultural task if he were to put the game away. The challenge for Team Romney was finding a dramatic way to convert the litany of alarming objective facts into plot points. It wasn't hard to agree that America was experiencing an economic crisis; what was difficult for the Republican campaign was to construct Romney as the hero who could make the crisis go away. Looking back on the election season, former presidential speech writer and *Wall Street Journal* columnist Peggy Noonan reflected upon the situation in mid-summer: "Mr. Romney couldn't articulate a way forward, and nobody knew what his presidency would look like."[40] The US electorate constituted the audience for political performance. For them to proclaim a hero, a compelling narrative of the future was required. If elected, how would the new president act in a dramatic and transformative way?

At the end of June, one of the most controversial policies of Obama's early presidency surged back into the limelight. In the preceding four months, the Supreme Court had entertained a strenuous challenge to the Affordable Care Act. It was widely feared, among those on the left, that the Roberts-led Republican majority on the court would vote to strike the Act down. Unexpectedly, the Supreme Court upheld the Affordable

Care Act as constitutional. In a 5–4 ruling marked by conservative Chief Justice John Roberts joining the court's four liberals, the majority declared that the so-called "individual mandate" was a tax that Congress could legitimately impose. Obama responded by emphasizing security and equality: "Whatever the politics, today's decision was a victory for people all over this country whose lives are more secure because of this law."[41] Romney simply denigrated the Act: "Obamacare was bad policy yesterday; it's bad policy today. Obamacare was bad law yesterday; it's bad law today."[42] A spate of opinion polls in the days following revealed that Americans remained divided on Obamacare and the Supreme Court decision.[43] If the court had declared the Act unconstitutional, however, the polluting power of the Tea Party's symbolic victory in the early struggle over healthcare might well have become part of the presidential campaign.

Every compelling plot has twists and turns. In early July, Romney unwittingly performed as a true blue member of the leisure class. Reporting on the Republican's family vacation on his New Hampshire estate, the *New York Times* described him "roaring across Lake Winnipesaukee on a powerboat large enough to hold two dozen members of his family."[44] For his part, Barack Obama made what were to become the most ill-fated comments of the summer. Speaking at a campaign event in Roanoke, Virginia, on July 13, the president elaborated upon the ways in which "wealthy, successful Americans" had "help" along the way:

> [L]ook, if you've been successful, you didn't get there on your own. You didn't get there on your own. I'm always struck by people who think, well, it must be because I was just so smart. There are a lot of smart people out there. It must be because I worked harder than everybody else. Let me tell you something – there are a whole bunch of hardworking people out there. [Applause.][45]

Obama's aim was to justify higher taxes on the wealthy and government programs for those who were not – by evoking the breadth and importance of social solidarity. But he pushed collective obligation so far that his remarks could be construed as threatening the sacred democratic tenet of individual autonomy.

> If you were successful, somebody along the line gave you some help. There was a great teacher somewhere in your life. Somebody helped to create this unbelievable American system that we have that allowed you to thrive. Somebody invested in roads and bridges. If you've got a business – you didn't build that. Somebody else made that happen. The Internet didn't get invented on its own. Government research created the Internet so that all the companies could make money off the Internet.[46]

Romney seized on the phrase "you didn't build that" and accused the president of insulting individuals who had indeed built businesses, beginning with the mythical icons of capitalist lore: "The idea to say that Steve Jobs didn't build Apple, that Henry Ford didn't build Ford Motor, that Papa John didn't build Papa John's Pizza," he declaimed, "it is not just foolishness. It's insulting to every entrepreneur, every innovator in America, and it's wrong. I find it extraordinary that a philosophy of that nature would be spoken by a president of the United States."[47] Within days, a television ad aired that opened with the president's remarks and featured an earnest business owner asking some pointed questions:

> My father's hands didn't build this company? My hands didn't build this company? My son's hands aren't building this company? Did somebody else take out the loan on my father's house that financed the equipment? Did somebody else make payroll every week and figure out where it's coming from? ... Through hard

work and a little luck, we built this business. Why are you demonizing us for it?[48]

Obama was quick to point out that his remarks were taken out
of context, averring in a new spot airing in six battleground
states: "Of course Americans build their own businesses."[49] But
performance is all about contingency. The president's ill-formed
words could not be taken back. They had struck a dangerously
negative chord, seeming to put him on the wrong side of sacred
morality. Republican surveys suggested the remarks had pro-
voked an "emotional response" among voters, disturbing those
"in nearly every demographic."[50]

The "you didn't build that" exchange spoke to the very nature
of American collective identity, to the slippery yet powerful connection of civil with national culture. Throughout the summer,
accusations of not understanding the essence of America
bounced back and forth between the candidates, though they
were shrouded in comments about jobs or the economy. The
Obama campaign hammered on the issue of class, continuing
its push to portray Romney as a one-percenter completely out
of touch with ordinary Americans, not to mention that he kept
secret foreign bank accounts and sent American jobs abroad.
Against a backdrop video of Romney providing a monotone
rendition of "America the Beautiful," an Obama campaign ad
broadcast a barrage of news bytes about outsourcing jobs, Swiss
bank accounts, and offshore tax havens.[51] Obama's point was
that Romney stood for a part, but not the whole, for narrow
interest at the expense of the broader solidarity of a democratic
civil sphere.

Romney's response was revealing. He claimed solidarity with
small business owners, suggesting it was they who represented
the true heart of the nation. As a *Wall Street Journal* columnist put it: "Few things better symbolize the average American
than a small-business owner. To the extent that Mr. Romney is

positioning himself as champion of that little business guy and portraying Mr. Obama as something alien, he could flip the Obama narrative on its head."[52] At a town hall event, Romney tried to make this potentially deeply polluting idea hit home. Citing Obama's phrase "you didn't build that," the Republican suggested it "really reveals what he thinks about our country, about our people, about free enterprise, about freedom, about individual initiative, about America."[53] John H. Sununu, former New Hampshire governor, White House chief of staff in the first Bush administration and ardent supporter of Romney, sought to underscore this stigmatizing effort in what some observers understood as a racial manner. "I wish this president would learn how to be an American," Sununu avowed, a remark he would later seek to clarify: "What I thought I said but I guess I didn't say is that the president has to learn the American formula for creating business."[54] Not being comfortable with the language of business, Republicans were betting, would push Obama outside the boundaries of the American civil sphere.

The issue of being American enough also played out along the boundary that connected domestic politics with foreign affairs. Already back in 2010, in his book *No Apology*, Romney had portrayed the president as going around the world apologizing for America, an assertion he repeated in a 2011 primary debate in Orlando, Florida. After the president entered into military myth for killing bin Laden, it became much more difficult for the Republican to launch this kind of attack. In an apparent effort to overcome this unexpected barrier, Romney set off overseas, determined to showcase his abilities with regard to foreign relations. The script was well written, but the political actor's performance turned out to be far from assured. Romney faltered from the outset, in each country making comments that bounced back to undermine his efforts to present himself as a confident, intelligent leader. On the eve of the 30th Olympiad in London, Romney insulted his ideological compatriot, Conservative Prime Minister David Cameron, questioning the UK's readiness to host a successful event: "It's hard to know just how well it will turn out. There are a few things that were disconcerting – the stories about the private security firm not having enough people, the supposed strike of the immigration and customs officials – that obviously is not something which is encouraging."[55] Cameron's retort the next day was brusque: "We are holding an Olympic Games in one of the busiest, most active, bustling cities anywhere in the world. Of course it's easier if you hold an Olympic Games in the middle of nowhere," referring to the Utah Olympics that Romney had been in charge of a decade earlier.[56] On the second stop of his foreign policy trip, Romney offended Palestinians by invoking "culture" as a reason for their wealth disparity with Israel: "Culture makes all the difference. . . . As you come here and you see the G.D.P. per capita, for instance, in Israel, which is about $21,000, and compare that with the G.D.P. per capita just across the areas managed by the Palestinian Authority, which is more like $10,000 per capita, you notice such a dramatically stark difference in economic vitality."[57] And although Romney was otherwise welcomed warmly in Poland, its historic trade union Solidarity, which had led the momentous fight against Communist rule three decades before, sharply distanced itself from the Republican: "Regretfully, we were informed by our friends from the American headquarters of [trade union federation] AFL-CIO . . . that Mitt Romney supported attacks on trade unions and employees' rights . . . Solidarity was not involved in organizing Romney's meeting with [former president and Solidarity leader] Walesa and did not invite him to visit Poland."[58]

News outlets on both sides of the Atlantic referred to Romney's trip as full of "missteps" and "gaffes." The major German weekly *Der Spiegel* headlined "Tour de Gaffes," saying, "He's only been abroad for a week, but the Palestinians are accusing him of racism, the Brits are annoyed and Polish union leaders don't like him."[59] A *Washington Post* editorial dubbed the trip "Gaffepalooza."[60] Even the conservative and business-oriented French newspaper *Le Figaro* asked, "Is Mitt Romney a loser?"[61] Britain's conservative tabloid, *The Sun*, dubbed him "Mitt the Twit."[62] It didn't help matters any that, after reporters barraged him with questions about how poorly the trip was going, a Romney aide told reporters to "shove it" and "kiss my ass."[63] Apologies followed, but blaming the messenger for the message is a sure sign of failed performance. The Democrats described Romney's foreign trip as a dramatic failure: "Romney was auditioning to be leader of the free world, and it's clear he was simply unable to represent America on the world stage," a senior campaign adviser proclaimed, emphasizing the performance's failure to connect: "It is clear that the opportunity to credential his beliefs with the American voters was nothing short for Mitt Romney of an embarrassing disaster on this trip."[64] Even the Republican side conceded that the trip had been a calamity, with a member of Romney's national finance committee describing it as "a mistake from beginning to end."[65] The failed performance may have finally disrupted the stalemate in the election polls. Although Nate Silver's forecast shifted only slightly, several national level polls now showed Obama leading Romney by a margin of 7–10 points.[66] Headlining "A bad July for Romney," Sam Wang noted a change in the margin of 3 points in Obama's favor for the month.[67]

When he returned to the relatively safer haven of the US, Romney resumed his assault on Obama's character, this time in a specifically religious way. In early August, the campaign released an ad chastising an Affordable Care Act provision mandating employers to cover contraception for women. Utilizing a backdrop from Romney's recent stop in Poland, followed by stills of Pope John Paul II and video of Lech Walesa endorsing the Republican candidate, the ad asked pointedly:

[Narrator]: Who shares your values? President Obama used his health care plan to declare war on religion, forcing religious institutions to go against their faith. Mitt Romney believes that's wrong. [Romney voice over]: In 1979, a son of Poland, Pope John Paul the Second, spoke words that would bring down an empire: "Be not afraid." [Narrator]: When religious freedom is threatened, who do you want to stand with?[68]

Romney was describing himself as the defender of religion; yet, by concluding with the concept of religious freedom, Romney crossed back from the religious to the civil sphere, planting his foot firmly on the side of sacred American values.

Later that month, both candidates seized another opportunity to intertwine politics and religion in parallel interviews with *Cathedral Age Magazine,* a publication of Washington National Cathedral. In the face of Romney's religious challenge, Obama was unusually explicit about his personal beliefs, presenting his religious conviction as a compelling political qualification: "First and foremost, my Christian faith gives me a perspective and security that I don't think I would have otherwise: That I am loved. That, at the end of the day, God is in control." However, the Democrat immediately followed up with a statement that balanced religious commitment and civil obligations, asserting that faith alone could not be used to take a candidate's measure: "Faith can express itself in people in many ways, and I think it is important that we not make faith alone a barometer of a person's worth, value, or character." In response, Romney withdrew from defining religion as a litmus test for office, placing his religion squarely within the civil sphere: "Perhaps the most important question to ask a person of faith who seeks a political office is whether he or she shares these American values: the equality of human kind, the obligation to serve one another, and a steadfast commitment to liberty. They are not unique to any one denomination."[69]

On August 11, Romney had made known his decision to choose Congressman Paul Ryan as his vice-presidential running mate. The choice was clearly directed at the conservative seats in America's political theater, especially the grass-roots Republican activists whose relation with Romney had always been rocky and whom he was finding it increasingly difficult to fire up with enthusiasm for his campaign. This audience was indeed thrilled with Ryan's nomination. The darling of the Tea Party[70] was a leader of the right-wing House bloc that had stirred up so much trouble for Obama after the Republicans seized control in the election of November, 2010. It was Ryan who had supplied the fuel, the framework, and the numbers for the budget-slashing right-wing budget proposal against which Obama had campaigned so passionately since the spring of 2011.

Weekly Standard editor and Fox News commentator Fred Barnes opined in the *Wall Street Journal* that, "With his big ideas, the GOP's vice presidential candidate makes the incumbent president seem smaller." Barnes's statement, however, was more rhetorical hope than empirical description. He wanted his readers to believe that casting Ryan as the VP nominee would allow the congressman to become a central protagonist in the Republican campaign, shifting it in a more conservative, less centrist-leaning direction. Describing Ryan as a "central figure" in the race, Barnes declared that the emergence of "The Ryan effect" had "turned the race upside down."[71] "*Ryan psychs Obama out,*" declared the neo-imperialist, right-leaning Harvard historian Niall Ferguson, who went on to explain in his *Newsweek* column: "The reason he psychs him out is that, unlike Obama, Ryan has a plan – as opposed to a narrative – for this country."[72] The *Wall Street Journal*, clearly overjoyed, eagerly reported that the Ryan choice produced not only plaudits from the right-wing critics who mediate political performances for conservative audiences, but immediate, highly tangible results: "Gov. Romney's poll numbers ticked up in Ohio and Virginia, both swing states. His online fundraising shot up like a geyser (68% of it coming from new donors). The Romney Facebook page added 510,000 friends in five days."[73] *Red State*'s Dan Spencer headlined "Romney's magnificent Ryan roll out" and noted that the "very good choice" had "energized the Conservative base and the TEA Party wing of the Republican coalition."[74]

All of this was day dreaming, the Republican version of Freud's wish-fulfillment for the individual psyche. Much like McCain's choice of Sarah Palin four years earlier, Ryan's nomination was a case of strong performance, narrow audience. It generated an arena of symbolic and emotional fusion that, while successful on a small scale, actually generated failure on the broader stage. In terms of the latter, the performance boomeranged, making it much more difficult for the newly coupled Republican ticket to connect with audiences more moderate than the right.

In fact, the Republican casting of Paul Ryan as protagonist projected the very same political story on which Obama had successfully performed symbolic jujitsu throughout 2011. After the right came to power in the House in January, 2011, the president had lain in wait for the "Ryan Budget," pouncing when it emerged in cold hard print. It was Obama's dramatic opposition to the budget that had allowed him to contrast his new narrative of growth from the middle out against elitist trickle down. President Obama had managed to transform an arcane budget fight into a struggle over the heart of the civil sphere, countering conservative austerity for the mass of Americans with a script demanding shared sacrifice and cross-class solidarity. The performance had allowed the struggling president to fire up his narrative and begin to redeem his heroic status. As poll numbers showed the Democrat pulling away from the Republican House in popularity and trustworthiness, his performance had destroyed the cultural power of the Tea Party.

Now, facing right across from him in the presidential campaign, was the very man who had authored that earlier, and failed, Republican script. It was the *New York Times*, not the *Weekly Standard* or the *Wall Street Journal*, that had it right: Romney's vice-presidential choice would provide the Obama campaign with "a bigger target"[75] for its political campaign. Political pundits on all sides were surprised when the toughest poll analyst in town, the *New York Times*'s Nate Silver, published his findings that the Ryan choice had generated, at most, a 1–2-point bounce for the Republican campaign, well below average for presidential candidates after selecting a running mate.[76] For Obama, Paul Ryan was truly the gift that kept on giving.

Ryan's new visibility allowed the Democrats to expand their charges against Romney as a one-percenter into a broad, easily communicated indictment of the Republican campaign's proposals for changing the nation's social policies. The pivotal issue in this broadening was Medicare. The raging, decades-long debate over "the future of Medicare" represented a fundamental ideological argument about America's political and economic organization. How much equality should governments guarantee? What should the size and role of the government in a democratic society be? An ad from the Obama campaign suggested that his opponents' commitment to cutting government healthcare represented favoritism to the wealthy: "Romney–Ryan: ending Medicare as we know it. To pay for a tax cut for millionaires and billionaires."[77] Meanwhile, the other side sought to offer reassurance to older Americans, a major Republican voting bloc: "The Romney Ryan plan protects Medicare benefits for today's seniors and strengthens the plan for the next generation."[78] Deploying a familiar narrative strategy, each campaign sought to link this specific issue to the hinge of history. "More than any other election, this is a choice about two different visions for the country, for two different directions of where America should go," Obama warned at a campaign stop in Chicago. In Virginia the day before, Ryan had intoned, "We're in a different, and dangerous, moment."[79]

6

Pulling Ahead

Just before the party conventions in late August, 2012, an Associated Press GfK poll suggested that 23 percent of potential voters were still "persuadable." Either they hadn't determined whom to back or they didn't have a strong feeling about their preferred candidate.[1] For this still not yet fully committed group, there would be much choosing and weighting in the home stretch.

The parties' back-to-back presidential nominating conventions – long shorn of decision-making power because of competitive primaries – featured two made-for-TV scripts. The Republican performance, which unrolled first, narrated the winner-take-all and the rest be damned ethic of the GOP's ex-businessman nominee. Despite his conservative credentials, *Times* columnist David Brooks bitterly remarked upon the "hyper-individualism" of the Republican performance: "Speaker after speaker celebrated the solitary and heroic individual. There was almost no talk of community and compassion."[2] Peggy Noonan, too, reflected on how the speakers were "too entrepreneurial – they were in business for themselves. They told their own stories, lauded their own history – a whole lot of I, I, I."[3]

The week-long Democratic convention that followed continuously evoked the all-for-one-and-one-for-all ethos of its former community organizer nominee. Obama declared:

We, the people – recognize that we have responsibilities as well as rights; that our destinies are bound together; that a freedom which asks only, what's in it for me, a freedom without a commitment to others, a freedom without love or charity or duty or patriotism, is unworthy of our founding ideals, and those who died in their defense. . . . We don't turn back. We leave no one behind. We pull each other up. We draw strength from our victories. And we learn from our mistakes. But we keep our eyes fixed on that distant horizon knowing that providence is with us and that we are surely blessed to be citizens of the greatest nation on earth.[4]

The president reiterated the urgency of a nation sitting on the hinge of history: "You will face the clearest choice of any time in a generation."[5]

By this time, political commentators and pollsters were talking about an "empathy gap." In its August update to donors, the Republican campaign warned that "voters believe Obama is more relatable."[6] A Republican software consultant confided to journalists, "Romney gives the impression that he is totally disconnected from normal people."[7] According to news reports, Romney's advisors were "feverishly working for ways to persuade voters that even though Romney is not like them, he can still relate to their lives."[8] Over the coming weeks, the Republican campaign pledged to "strengthen its connection with voters." In the beginning of September, in the crucial battleground state of Ohio, the president had an 18 percent lead over the Republican on the issue of "who cares more about your problems."[9]

The nominating convention failed to yield much of a bounce in the polls for Romney – below average by historical standards.[10] In fact, Sam Wang reported that the Republican convention resulted in a negative bounce, with the popular vote margin moving toward Obama by one point.[11] As for the Obama camp, they had much to celebrate. According to Nate

Silver, even before the end of their convention, after speeches by Michelle Obama and Bill Clinton, the polls already reflected a 2–3-point bounce.[12] The president's approval ratings – recording his job performance – were finally catching up with his personal favorability ratings.[13] After the close of the festivities, polls now gave Obama a 3–5 point lead, with some reporting as high as 8–9 points difference.[14] In reporting *FiveThirtyEight*'s meticulously constructed "now-cast" for the popular vote, Silver declared that Obama "went from being 1.4 percentage points ahead when his convention began, to four points ahead a week after it ended, once there had been time for it to work its way through the polls."[15]

The killing of four Americans at the Libyan embassy on September 11 brought foreign policy to the surface in what, for Obama, seemed a potentially troubling way. A president must appear capable of defending the civil sphere from national enemies. In his deft response to the embassy murders, Obama sent a message that brashly intertwined military might with a sturdy defense of democratic values.

> So what I want all of you to know is that we are going to bring those who killed our fellow Americans to justice. I want people around the world to hear me: To all those who would do us harm, no act of terror will go unpunished. It will not dim the light of the values that we proudly present to the rest of the world. No act of violence shakes the resolve of the United States of America.[16]

Romney tried countering Obama's performance by painting the president as an apologist for America. In their initial response to the killings, American diplomats had not only condemned the terrorist acts but also criticized the inflammatory US-produced Web film that, in denouncing Islam, had appeared to be the catalyst for the violence. Romney jumped on what he claimed to be the apologetic character of the president's remarks: "It's disgraceful that the Obama administration's first response was not to condemn attacks on our diplomatic missions, but to sympathize with those who waged the attacks."[17] Two days later, he widened his critique, declaring that the president had lost control of foreign events, becoming supine: "As we watch the world today, sometimes it seems that we're at the mercy of events, instead of shaping events, and a strong America is essential to shape events."[18] As a survey taken the following week revealed, some in the center section of the American audience agreed. The president's job performance on foreign affairs dropped to 49 percent, a 5-point drop from the month before and the first time it had fallen below 50 percent since April 2011, just before the president announced the death of Osama bin Laden.[19] This small shift, however, didn't change the horserace – Obama retained his lead.[20]

It wasn't long before attention snapped back to the economy. Again, the connection to being the best American possible surfaced. Speaking to veterans in Virginia and in a two-minute ad, Obama focused on a new mode of patriotism, one in which national pride depended on economic equality and social solidarity: "It's time for a new economic patriotism, rooted in the belief that growing our economy begins with a strong thriving middle class."[21] Obama positioned Romney as against equality and solidarity. Romney's swift response claimed that true economic patriotism meant reducing the nation's growing debt. A campaign spokesperson declared: "Four years ago, Barack Obama called it 'unpatriotic' to run up debts our children will have to pay. Yet in the time it takes his latest ad to run, our national debt grows by at least another $5 million."[22] A television ad focusing on environmental curbs on the coal industry accused the president of "waging war on coal, while we lose jobs to China."[23]

With Obama now clearly ahead in most polls, and with a 4.1 percentage point lead in Nate Silver's now-cast for the popular vote,[24] an utterly unexpected moment of highly charged drama burst onto the public stage. The leftist magazine *Mother Jones* posted grainy, film-noir like footage of Mitt Romney speaking at a $50,000-a-head fundraiser at a home in Boca Raton, Florida. What would come to be known as the "47 percent" remark immediately went viral, with two million views by the next day.[25] The secretly recorded, ill-fated words would resonate throughout the rest of the campaign:[26]

> There are 47 percent of the people who will vote for the president no matter what. All right, there are 47 percent who are with him, who are dependent upon government, who believe that they are victims, who believe the government has a responsibility to care for them, who believe that they are entitled to health care, to food, to housing, to you-name-it. That that's [*sic*] an entitlement. And the government should give it to them. And they will vote for this president no matter what . . . These are people who pay no income tax.[27]

Painting this less privileged half of the American citizen audience as dependent and devoid of individual responsibility, Romney wrote them off as possible partners in democratic deliberation: "My job is, is not to worry about those people. I'll never convince them they should take personal responsibility and care for their lives."[28] To become a collective symbol of democracy, a political figure must be seen as inclusive. To be truly civil, a society must be a place where everyone gets a shot to belong. Potential voters must be coded as members, not outsiders. "It's hard to serve as president," Obama campaign manager Jim Messina immediately responded with a tweet, "when you've disdainfully written off half the nation."[29]

To make matters worse, as news outlet after news outlet pointed out, Romney's comments reflected a serious flaw of omission. Of the 46.4 percent of Americans who don't pay income taxes, two-thirds contribute in the form of payroll taxes – automatic withholdings for Social Security and Medicare. And a majority of the remaining third of the "47 percent" consists of retirees, who pay no tax because they do not report income.[30] It was, then, not only that Romney appeared as secretive and elitist, speaking disdainfully about half of the American population to super-rich supporters behind closed doors. He was also seen as dishonest, a trickster with statistics. Even conservative pundits who wanted Romney in the White House were putting him on the wrong side of the moral values that define for Americans what is good and right. William Kristol contributed an article to the *Weekly Standard* entitled "Note on Romney's Arrogant and Stupid Remarks."[31] The candidate's own running mate dubbed Romney's comments "inarticulate."[32]

Even as a Bloomberg News opinion editor was declaring, "Today, Mitt Romney lost the election,"[33] the Republican production team scrambled for a way to cauterize this possibly mortal wound. Aides organized a press conference later the same day, interrupting a fundraiser in Costa Mesa, California. But either the script was badly written or the candidate failed to perform in the expected way. Rather than apologizing, Romney doubled down. His statement seemed to suggest that his secretly recorded off-the-cuff observations actually represented his considered beliefs. He actually did believe half of the nation paid no taxes, that they were abjectly dependent on government, and that he would have to write them off as possible supporters of the Republican campaign.

> I recognize that among those that pay no tax ... I'm not likely to be highly successful with the message of lowering taxes. That's not as attractive to those who don't pay income taxes as it is to those who do. And likewise those who are reliant on government are not as attracted to my message of slimming down the size of government.[34]

Seizing what he apparently viewed as a golden opportunity
for moral clarity, Romney linked the supposed dependency of
America's lower half to the character of his Democratic opponent, equating Obama's support for government programs with
being an enemy of freedom:

> The president and I have very different approaches to the future of
> America and what it takes to ignite our economy and put people
> back to work. The president believes in what I've described as a
> government centered society . . . and I happen to believe instead in
> a free enterprise, free-individual society.[35]

Extraordinarily maladroit, this response failed entirely to
address widespread concern about the exclusionary elitism
of Romney's original performance, offering an open field for
Democratic performances that would. Felicitously seizing the
moment, the Democrats cited Romney's earlier remarks to reinforce what had now become one of its most important campaign slogans: "If Mitt Romney wins, the middle class loses."[36]
An ad produced by Priorities USA Action interspersed Romney's
recorded comments, and an image of the lavish Florida home
where he had made them, with a middle-class family's struggles behind the doors of a modest suburban house.[37] Another
spot, created by the Obama campaign, simply replayed Mitt
Romney's own words against a somber backdrop of black-and-
white stills of blue-collar workers, veterans, and families.[38] In
an appearance on the Late Show with David Letterman, the
president underscored his own commitment to the widest possible civil solidarity, describing all Americans, Democratic and
Republican, as fully capable individuals deserving of respect
and inclusion:

> [O]ne of the things I've learned as president is you represent the
> entire country. And when I meet Republicans as I'm traveling

around the country, they are hard working, family people, who care deeply about this country and my expectation is that if you want to be president you got to work for everybody not just for some.

As Obama continued, he countered what for millions of Americans was the most hurtful aspect of Romney's remarks – about the 47 percent being "victims." There was nothing wrong with giving and receiving help, the president insisted; rather, it was a sign of social solidarity.

> There are not a lot of people out there who think they're victims. There are not a lot of people who think they're entitled to something. What I think the majority of people, Democrats and Republicans, believe is that we've got some obligations to each other and there's nothing wrong with us giving each other a helping hand.[39]

On the campaign trail, the president hammered hard on Romney's remarks, calling his opponent "out of touch" and, in an engagingly colloquial style, presenting him as shut up in an elite world that shut out the average American: "When you express an attitude that half the country considers itself victims, that somehow they want to be dependent on government, my thinking is maybe you haven't gotten around a lot."[40]

In the days after the 47 percent remark went viral and flooded the press and airwaves, national polls reflected gains for Obama of anywhere from 5 to 8 points,[41] with Sam Wang's popular vote Meta-Margin hitting 5 percent as of September 26, the highest level thus far.[42] In two of the most hotly contested swing states, Ohio and Florida, Obama now had the lead by 9 and 10 points, respectively.[43] And a closer look showed that nearly half of "likely Romney voters" in Ohio (48 percent) "supported him with reservations or because they dislike Mr. Obama, compared with 51 percent who said they strongly favored him." In contrast, the president was "strongly favored by two-thirds

of his likely voters, with 33 percent saying they favor him
with reservations or because of dislike of Mr. Romney."[44] A
comment from a follow-up interview with one Florida respond-
ent reached behind the numbers, capturing how Romney's per-
sistent reluctance to be inclusive, to exhibit broad feelings of
solidarity, undercut the possibility of fusing with the American
audience: "There's just something about him I don't trust. It's
not so much that I don't believe what he is saying, but I just
don't think he's for the middle and lower class. He's more for
helping the rich."[45]

The episode of the "47 percent" became a darkly iconic
moment for Romney, not only, perhaps not even primarily,
because of what he actually said, but because of how these
remarks fit into a slowly developing dramatic frame. After
the near-death experience of the 2010 midterms, Obama had
been hanging by his proverbial fingernails. In the two years
following, he had pulled himself up from the political precipice,
skillfully scripting his Republican opponents, first the Congress
and then Mitt Romney, as cold hearted, mean-spirited, anti-
civil, and out of touch. When *Mother Jones* released the secret
recording, it immediately assumed the role of material artifact,
an archeological discovery that provided empirical evidence for
the Democratic president's rhetoric. Romney's remarks seemed
to demonstrate that what Obama had been saying for two years
was not a performance but an act of truth-telling, something
factually descriptive that was morally in the right. Even after
the revelation, the Republican candidate, rather than distancing
himself, performed in a manner that appeared to underscore the
accuracy of Obama's claims.

The cultural advantage Obama gained from this dramatic
moment began spilling over into perceptions of his acumen in
the economic domain.[46] A CBS/*New York Times* poll showed
Obama cutting into Romney's advantage "as the candidate
voters say is most likely to restore the economy and create

jobs."[47] And the *Wall Street Journal* reported that, "in the latest Wall Street Journal/NBC News poll, all the key swing groups – independents, moderates and those not firmly committed – say they think the president would do a better job handling the deficit than would Mr. Romney."[48]

7

Harrowing Home Stretch

Even as Obama's power to symbolize finally was translating into a significant electoral lead, difficult hurdles lay ahead. As compared with theater, the performance of politics cannot be fully scripted, nor can its mise-en-scène be thoroughly organized in advance. Politics is life, not art. It is filled with contingencies that can only be framed after the fact. The convulsions over "47 percent" were only beginning to die down when the political stage was being set for the next dramatic moment of the 2012 campaign – the first of the three presidential debates.

Ever since the legendary Lincoln–Douglas confrontations more than 150 years ago, widely publicized debates had served as a proving ground for presidential candidates.[1] From the time of the first modern presidential confrontations in 1960, between Kennedy and Nixon, political observers had considered them the beginning of the real presidential race. A veteran pollster for the NBC/*Wall Street Journal* survey recalled that, "for a lot of us who follow politics, the general election started after the conventions" with the series of three presidential debates, adding that he believed this remained the case for "a lot of these swing voters."[2] It was these still "persuadable" members of the citizen audience, who hovered around the center, that the debate performance of the Democratic president would have to reassure.

Albert Hunt of Bloomberg News wrote in the *New York Times* that "the very few game-changers in debates occur when a candidate makes a mistake or exposes an unattractive personality trait."[3] Hunt worried that Obama's "arrogance" and "scorn" for Romney might prove his undoing.[4] It was a prescient remark.

What the more than 70 million viewers[5] of the first debate on October 3 witnessed was a debacle for Team Obama. Struggling to match the newly moderate Romney's sharply brilliant performance, Obama seemed to revert to his "Rational Man" persona, the role that had made dramatic success impossible during the early years of his term. Obama focused on substance over style, choosing to highlight issues over inspired narratives, reluctant to aggressively engage in symbolic pollution – with the 47 percent remark, Bain Capital, Romney's personal tax situation, and his overseas investments never receiving a mention.

When the curtain went down, dismal reviews of Obama's debate performance came from every direction. One might expect a conservative pundit such as Peggy Noonan to announce "Romney Deflates the President."[6] And *Wall Street Journal* editorial board member James Taranto, unsurprisingly waxing negative too, musing "the Obama that guys like [liberal commentators] Matthews and Sullivan expected instead was a character in a fairy tale – a fairy tale written by guys like Matthews and Sullivan."[7] But even the *New York Times* had to admit defeat, reporting "a torrent of criticism directed at President Obama, with Republicans, and as well as many Democrats, accusing Mr. Obama of delivering a flat, uninspired and defensive performance."[8] Liberal commentators also let loose. Tweeting immediately after the debate, blogger Andrew Sullivan, a fervent Obama supporter, pointed to the infelicitous failures, exclaiming, "He's boring, abstract, and less human-seeming than Romney!" and describing the performance "a rolling calamity."[9] Comedian Bill Maher, who had very publicly donated $1 million to a super PAC supporting the president, tweeted an equally damning indictment: "I can't believe I'm saying this, but Obama looks like he DOES need a teleprompter."[10] The super-liberal MSNBC host Ed Shultz asked pointedly, "Where was the president tonight?"[11] The presidential debater seemed to have left the stage.

From the Obama camp, there were shrugs of defeat as they fielded what the *Wall Street Journal* described as "a deluge of complaints" from donors and supporters.[12] Stephanie Cutter, the Democrats' deputy campaign manager, told CNN that Romney "scores points on style."[13] Though he had looked ashen and shell-shocked in the immediate aftermath of Obama's debacle, David Axelrod artfully tried to recover the following day, polluting Romney as an "artful dodger" whose comments were "devoid of honesty," "rooted in deception," "untethered to the truth," and "well delivered but fraudulent."[14] While the image-maker-in-chief grudgingly acknowledged that Romney "may win the Oscar for his performance last night," he maintained "he's not going to win the presidency."[15] Trying to make lemonade out of Obama's lemon, the campaign worked furiously to push the idea that Romney had broken one of democracy's most sacred commandments – no lying – and immediately produced a TV ad called "Trust" along with a series of six Web videos.[16] Senior advisor David Plouffe announced, "Going forward here, one of the things we're going to have to adjust to is that dishonesty."[17]

Apart from the narrow bandwidth of devotees, however, the campaign's efforts at interpretive mediation seemed like mere spinning, and they were. Political audiences declared Romney the winner of the debate both over the short and long term, from focus groups held during the debate[18] to the more enduring measure of polling. After a week of this, Nate Silver, in the *New York Times*'s FiveThirtyEight blog, reported the shocking news that Romney now seemed to be leading the president

– by an average of 4.6 percent, based on 15 individual polls. Although "it is not clear whether Mr. Romney is still gaining ground," Silver explained that, "unlike earlier, Mr. Romney is now seeing some of his best results in swing state polls" – "six of the seven polls published on Friday from such states had him ahead."[19] Even the ever-optimistic Sam Wang acknowledged a 4-point drop in his popular vote Meta-Margin.[20] In a spectacular headline, a Pew poll report declared, "Romney's Strong Debate Performance Erases Obama's Lead." Pew's survey showed that, among likely voters, Obama's pre-debate 8-point lead had now become a 4 percent deficit, and that Romney's favorability rating now matched the president's.[21] The gap in the respondents' views of who had done a better job in the debate was dramatic – Romney far outpaced the president, 66 percent vs. 20 percent.[22] One of the widely remarked appeals of the Romney character that Americans witnessed during the debate was the tacking toward the center.[23] According to Pew, swing voters had shifted to Romney by 5 points and now gave him a 10-point advantage in the category "has new ideas" (39 vs. 29 percent).[24] Reminding Americans about the hinge of history, Romney called the debate an "important night for the country."[25] Vice-presidential hopeful Ryan followed in tandem: "Last night we saw a clear picture, we saw a clear choice."[26]

Even as his "style points" were earned for aggressiveness,[27] the newly moderate Romney performance also managed to reveal his "softer side." Appearing on Sean Hannity's Fox News show, the post-debate Romney finally apologized for the 47 percent remark: "I said something that's just completely wrong. My life has shown that I care about 100 percent."[28] The *New York Times* reported that, "appearing buoyed by his widely acclaimed debate performance, the Romney on display this week was a looser, more relaxed one.[29]

Team Obama's script for the subsequent debates was to become more "aggressive,"[30] the candidate suggesting that, during the first performance, he had been "too polite."[31] The president took off the gloves for the second debate on October 16, matching Romney blow-by-blow in what body language expert Patti Wood described as "one of the most physical debates . . . in terms of candidates' posturing": "Absolutely . . . at times almost frightening. Because they were circling each other at times like they were prey. There was sword fighting with gestures. There was gun pointing. It was very intense. I've never seen anything like it and I've been doing this kind of analysis for over thirty years."[32] As one editor at the *Wall Street Journal* put it, "If you turn down the volume you would've thought you were watching the Nature Channel."[33] According to the *New York Times*, Obama and Romney "circled each other like tomcats in an alley."[34] Media coverage was intensely focused on combat metaphors, reaching for terms like "battle,"[35] "head-to-head,"[36] "fight,"[37] "attack,"[38] and "pugilistic."[39] The *Los Angeles Times*'s Jon Healy said the debate "played more like a brutal exchange of punches between heavyweights, ending with both men battered but standing. Intense throughout, even riveting at times, it was fantastic theater – but not decisive politics."[40]

To the contrary, in this theatrical confrontation great political power was at stake. The studio audience, which had provided the questions for the second debate, was composed of those undecided or open to changing their mind – the persuadable voters.[41] It was precisely these voters whom Obama sought to convince that Romney was actually a lot more conservative than he had wished to appear in the first debate.[42] The president succeeded. In an instant reaction poll conducted by CBS News of uncommitted voters watching the second debate, 37 percent thought Obama won, compared to 30 percent for Romney,[43] a reversal of the first debate (Romney 46 percent vs. 22 percent for Obama).[44] Among the broader universe of voters, polls gave Obama an advantage in the debate performance of somewhere between 7 and 15 points. The president's comeback performance stopped Romney's first-debate momentum in its tracks. If Obama's second performance had also nosedived, there would have been hell to pay.

Exactly how this symbolic triumph translated into electoral predictions was, however, difficult to ascertain. According to Nate Silver, Obama had already regained some momentum before the second debate.[45] Similarly, Sam Wang declared that the "Ro-mentum" had stopped on October 13 – or even earlier.[46] The president's regained traction could have been caused by the short half-life of Romney's first debate aura, but it could also have been related to positive economic news.[47] With just one month to go in the campaign, the unemployment rate unexpectedly dropped to its lowest level since the president took office, falling to 7.8 percent for September 2012.[48] Whatever the reasons – and there is no doubt that Obama's restored performance was one of the most significant among them – by the time national electoral polls had weighed in after the second debate, Obama had demolished Romney's advantage and had an average lead of one-half a percentage point, 0.8 according to Nate Silver's forecast, and 1.8 according to Sam Wang.[49] Wang asserted that the third debate wouldn't play much of a role: "The cake's ingredients are mostly in. And the cake's in the oven."[50] He was right.

The final debate on October 22, addressing foreign policy, was accompanied by much less fanfare than the first two. Symbolic inversion no longer appeared imminent, and the political battle competed with two athletic ones, Monday Night Football and Game 7 of baseball's National League Championship Series. At stake in the debate was how the two candidates would enact the leadership role of protecting the nation. Romney's campaign, heading into the debate, painted his opponent as a failure and the nation as hanging on the edge: "America stands weakened around the world, with our safety threatened, our allies increasingly isolated, and hostile nations emboldened."[51] In his own pre-debate remarks, Obama's senior advisor David Plouffe signaled how the campaign would sculpt the president's image: "People want strength, and these are big issues about how we're going to stay safe, and how we're going to stay strong, and how we're going to lead the world."[52]

The viewing public witnessed another aggressive match-up. The *Wall Street Journal* declared it a "duel."[53] The *New York Times* reported that:

> [while] the debate broke little new ground, [it had] underscored that the differences between the two men on foreign policy rest more on tone, style and their sense of leadership than on particular policies … While they varied in degree, the heart of their clash rested on who would pursue the same national goals more effectively and ensure America's enduring economic and security role overseas.[54]

The *Wall Street Journal* agreed that the difference between the two men was "mainly one of tone."[55] Each candidate worked assiduously to paint the other in dark colors, with Obama implying Romney's leadership would be "reckless" and "all over the map," and Romney intertwining the foreign with the economic boundary of the civil sphere: "I look around the world, I don't see our influence growing around the world. I see our influence receding, in part because of the failure of the president to deal with our economic challenges at home."[56] The debate ended with each candidate shifting tack back to domestic issues. The president emphasized forward movement for the nation, claiming Romney would drive the country backward into disaster:

> You know, over the last four years, we've made real progress digging our way out of policies that gave us two prolonged wars, record deficits and the worst economic crisis since the Great Depression. And Governor Romney wants to take us back to those policies: a

foreign policy that's wrong and reckless; economic policies that won't create jobs, won't reduce our deficit, but will make sure that folks at the very top don't have to play by the same rules that you do.[57]

Romney countered by scripting the last four years as moving in reverse: "America's going to come back ... Washington is broken. I know what it takes to get this country back."[58]

Instant reaction polling to this third debate reported Obama as achieving a wide margin of victory among the crucial bloc of undecided voters – 30 points[59] – while polling of voters in general showed margins of 8 to 11 percent.[60]

With just two weeks to go to the election, Obama had regained the advantage. After Romney's peak in *FiveThirtyEight*'s "now-cast" a week after the first debate, when Obama's chances of winning the Electoral College had gone down to 61.1 percent,[61] the president's chances now stood back up at 71 percent[62] Sam Wang's model was far more sanguine: "In a race today, President Obama would win with about 90% probability."[63] Nonetheless, several widely respected polls still showed the candidates in a statistical dead heat.[64] The campaign's dramatic tension would be sustained.

The candidates now turned their attention to battleground states and intensified their symbolic efforts at mutual denigration. Each team furiously produced television, radio, and Web ads, many directed at Ohio, which according to Nate Silver was "central enough in the electoral math that it now seems to matter as much as the other 49 states put together."[65] Romney, who professed to believe he was slowly but steadily eroding Obama's lead in the state among likely voters,[66] spent four out of the five days after the final debate in Ohio.[67] Whatever Romney may have accomplished, however, was vaporized by yet another of his increasingly desperate campaign team's rhetorical missteps. In one of their most controversial ads of the campaign, "Who Will Do More?," a narrator spoke ominously against a visual backdrop of cars being crushed: "Obama took GM and Chrysler into bankruptcy, and sold Chrysler to Italians who are going to build Jeeps in China. Mitt Romney will fight for every American job."[68] The statement could be construed as accurate only in the most narrowly technical sense. Jeep would indeed build jeeps in China, but only for the Chinese market, while the firm would continue its US production for the rest of the world. In terms of the bigger picture, the ad was deeply misleading. Jobs would not be moved from Ohio to China and, while Obama had taken GM and Chrysler into a carefully controlled bankruptcy, his administration's guidance had ensured they would emerge from it far stronger. Indeed, Chrysler issued a tart and immediate response to the ad's claims, blogging that it displayed "a leap that would be difficult even for professional circus acrobats"[69] and emailing its employees to "unambiguously restate our position: Jeep production will not be moved from the United States to China."[70]

The Obama campaign, meanwhile, reminded viewers of Romney's adamant desire, expressed in his November 18, 2008, op-ed "Let Detroit Go Bankrupt," that the auto industry go belly-up.[71] Their ad, "Collapse," also highlighted the inaccuracy of Romney's outsourcing claim, condemning the Republican's moral character with this slashing verdict: "Mitt Romney on Ohio jobs? Wrong then. Dishonest Now."[72] The president barnstormed through Ohio reinforcing this message. "That's not true," he exclaimed, addressing a sympathetic crowd chanting "liar" and "lying." The president's wording was colloquial, but his outrage was unmistakable: "Everybody knows it's not true. The car companies themselves have told Governor Romney to knock it off."[73]

Such symbolics enhanced Obama's already substantial cultural power and further dissipated Romney's already diminished aura. Despite some pollsters still calling the race a toss-up,

Nate Silver pointed out the "simple case for saying Obama is the favorite": "Mr. Obama is leading in the polls of Ohio and other states that would suffice for him to win 270 electoral votes, and by a margin that has historically translated into victory a fairly high percentage of the time."[74] Sam Wang's snapshot also reflected a decisive win, with 297 electoral votes for Obama.[75] From mid-August onward, Obama had pulled ahead, gaining momentum from the blowback against Ryan, the strikingly contrasting conventions, and the iconic "47 percent." One *New York Times* op-ed columnist put it, "After the conventions, Romney was toast."[76] The president's dramatic breakdown in the first debate had threatened to capsize his campaign ship, but powerful showings in debates two and three had allowed him to recover his stride. It was now his election to lose.

On October 29, the force of nature created one final dramatic opportunity for the performers in the campaign. As Hurricane Sandy wreaked havoc up and down the Atlantic seaboard, both teams suspended their activities, with their strategists wondering whether people stuck at home would watch campaign ads and how those ads might look interspersed with images of people suffering from the storm.[77] Not only journalists but many Democratic handlers saw the natural disaster as possibly a political disaster for the president. Government responses to natural events are extraordinarily complicated, the particulars of federal agency decisions often not under presidential control, and those of local government even less so. Memories were still fresh about Hurricane Katrina bringing down Obama's White House predecessor, George W. Bush. Both candidates duly expressed their concern for the areas likely to be affected, and the media geared up for sensationalizing every moment of the coming storm, the natural and political both.

In the event, the president seized the opportunity, wrapping himself in the cloak of charisma that attaches to effective performance of office in times of social crisis and strain. In the eye of the storm, Obama exuded calm competence, even as he reached outward to embrace victims in what most observers depicted as emotional and affecting ways. This powerfully dramatic performance seemed to fill the storm area's geographical and figurative space, constructing a symbolic barrier that Romney could not penetrate. With so much of life and limb at stake, the Republican did not want to be seen as merely political, as trying to steal the scene; Romney remained largely off stage, resigning himself to turning one Ohio campaign stop into a "storm-relief" event collecting canned goods and other supplies.[78]

What crystallized the candidates' contrasting hurricane performances was the completely unexpected political one-eighty by the leader of the state most affected by the storm. Earlier, New Jersey governor Christie had viciously dressed down the president, in his role as keynote speaker at the Republican National Convention and also, just days prior to the storm, at a Republican campaign rally in Virginia. Telling Obama "you've been living inside 1600 Pennsylvania Avenue for the last four years," Christie declared, "if you don't think you can change Washington from inside the White House, then let's give you the plane ticket back to Chicago you've earned." He described the president as "wandering around a dark room" looking for the "light switch of leadership."[79] After Christie had experienced Hurricane Sandy, however, the Republican governor's praise flowed like honey, saying the president had been "outstanding," "incredibly supportive," and "deserves great credit."[80] The image of Christie – whom the *New York Times* had once called the Republican side's "most aggressive campaigner"[81] – giving the president a grateful bear hug blanketed the national television screens. It projected a powerful symbol of Obama representing the interests of every American citizen in a non-partisan way. One could hardly have ordered up a more perfect image to encapsulate the President's 20-plus months of electoral strategy. As if to add frosting to this hurricane cake,

New York City mayor Bloomberg, a self-declared independent, formally endorsed the president's re-election bid after having remained very publicly undecided throughout the campaign. Bloomberg explained, according to the *New York Times*, that Obama's handling of Hurricane Sandy had "reshaped [my] thinking."[82] Predictably, Obama deflected this praise of himself by praising the altruism of his fellow citizens. "It reminds us that when disaster strikes, we see America at its best . . . All the petty differences that consume us in normal times somehow melt away. There are no Democrats or Republicans in a storm – just fellow Americans."[83]

Nate Silver's forecast after the storm favored Obama as better than an 80 percent favorite to win the Electoral College, as compared to 73 percent on October 29.[84] According to Silver, Obama had gained some ground in a "statistically meaningful" way over the last few days, an average of 1.5 percentage points in most national polls.[85] Most of the latter, however, played it safe. They focused on the margin of error and capitalized on selected polling reports, deploying sensational headlines and dramatic stories about how close the race remained: "The race is poised on a knife-edge,"[86] "All signs are . . . that this is going to be a true cliffhanger,"[87] "Nail-Biter in 3 Key Counties,"[88] "It may be one of the tightest presidential elections in history."[89] As the days to Election Day ticked down to the wire, each campaign portrayed its candidate as the favorite, painting the other's narrative scenario as "myth."[90] David Axelrod referred to Romney team's idea that its candidate was building up steam as "faux-mentum": "I don't think they have momentum now, and I don't think they have for a while."[91] Richard Beeson, political director for the Romney campaign, sought to discredit the Obama team's ground game, which was ostensibly racking up early votes in key states.[92]

But if imitation is indeed the sincerest form of flattery, then the shifting slogans of the Republicans' last days revealed concern that Obama had pulled ahead. From October 25 onward, Romney tried to appropriate the "change" slogan central to both of Obama's presidential campaigns. "These challenges are big challenges," Mr. Romney said. "This election is therefore a big choice. And America wants to see big changes, and we're gonna bring big changes to get America stronger again."[93] Obama's reply presented the restored American hero still working for change, even as he extended the deadline for success:

> So when I say ... I know what real change looks like, you've got cause to believe me because you've seen me fight for it, and you've seen me deliver it. You've seen the scars on me to prove it. You've seen the gray hair on my head to show you what it means to fight for change. And you've been there with me. And after all we've been through together, we can't give up now.[94]

Enough of the American audience believed him. He won walking away.

8

Demography, Money, and Social Media

From the moment polling places closed on the evening of November 6, and the surprising extent of Obama's victory became known, commentators dissecting exit polls and voting results announced that it was actually "demographics" that had determined the outcome of Obama's last campaign. "A demographic tidal wave became a Democratic tidal wave," proclaimed the *San Francisco Chronicle*.[1] NBC News commentators described Election Day as downright explosive: "What happened last night was a demographic time bomb that had been ticking and that blew up in GOP faces."[2] The demographer William H. Frey, of the Brookings Institution, described "a wake-up call that will echo through the decades."[3] And veteran journalist Jonathan Alter titled a chapter of his 448-page tome on Obama and the election, "Demography as Destiny."[4]

These and other mainstream media picked up on the fact – cause for worry to some Americans, for celebration to others – that Obama had received 80 percent of the non-white vote.[5] In a nation poised to reach majority minority status by mid-century, this statistic seemed to provide a transparent window on the 2012 election, whose outcome appeared, to many, otherwise difficult to understand. Paul Taylor, of the non-partisan Pew Research Center, seized hold of the simple argument in a most dramatic way: "The nonwhite vote has been growing – tick, tick, tick – slowly, steadily. Every four-year cycle the electorate gets a little bit more diverse. And it's going to continue. This is a very powerful demographic that's changing our politics and our destiny."[6] It was an easy matter to correlate these changes in the composition of population with the lopsided distribution of minority votes. Seventy-one percent of Hispanics voted for Obama, and only 27 percent for Romney. Among Asian Americans, Obama won 73 percent of the vote. He received 55 percent of the women's vote, 60 percent of youth, and 69 percent of Jewish.[7] He may even have increased his support from African Americans from the 2008 level of 95 percent.[8] Among the 5 percent of the nation who identified as gay, lesbian, or bisexual, Obama took 76 percent of the vote.[9]

As students learn in first year statistics, however, correlations are not causes. While it seems paradoxical, the voting patterns of demographically *identifiable* groups are not demographically *determined*. Demographic identity does not automatically create some material or cultural interest. Demographic voting is not born but made. The relationship between political leaders and social groups is open-ended, not preset by demographic identity. It is a matter of meaning-making. What stories do political leaders project to different social groups? How are these projections related to the morality of civil solidarity? How are they perceived by the audiences to whom they are aimed?

Our examination of Obama's presidency and his last campaign demonstrates that neither his successes nor his failures were determined by simple demography. The cultural work he energetically engaged in – his self-construction as symbol and narrative – always intervened, and that work was all about embodying the civil sphere. One finds scarcely any special pleading in the chapters of the Obama story; it is driven, rather, by the protagonist's ambition to become a collective representation of American democracy, an embodiment of the widest possible social solidarity. Obama sought to perform as an everyman, uniting rather than separating, writing himself into the mythical narrative of national totems who had brought classes, races, religions, ethnicities, regions, genders, and (more recently) sexualities into closer alignment.[10]

From the earliest markings Obama scratched on the national collective conscience – as the first African American editor of *Harvard Law Review*, then as the youthful author of *Dreams from My Father* – he presented himself as embodying the utopian ideals Americans shared across demographic lines. As he moved from one station in life to another, from community organizer, to law student, to constitutional law professor, and finally to earnest politician, he sought to convince ever wider audiences of Americans that, if they trusted him, he would help repair the nation's institutions so that its utopian dreams could become more real. This self-understanding explains the indignant response Obama's chief pollster made to post-election demography-as-destiny claims. Pointing to the force of "underlying values" – values that sustain fairness and social solidarity – he insisted that "the president's victory" was "a triumph of vision, not of demographics":

He won because he articulated a set of values that define an America that the majority of us wish to live in: A nation that makes the investments we need to strengthen and grow the middle class. A nation with a fair tax system, and affordable and excellent education for all its citizens. A nation that believes that we're most prosperous when we recognize that we are all in it together.[11]

The color of Obama's skin, his African father, his relative youth – all these were objective demographic facts. But it was Obama the story-teller – the writer, the politician, the public performer – who often succeeded, but sometimes failed, in weaving these facts into the American story of "liberty and justice for all." A light-skinned black man married to a darker skinned black woman, he received 39 percent of the white vote. Despite the demographic shifts that were supposed to have determined Obama's 2012 victory, this was in line with the performance of other Democratic candidates over the last 10 elections, which averaged 40.6 percent.[12] And, indeed, the African American president and candidate received not only the votes but the abiding admiration of tens of millions of these white voters besides.

As president, Obama was determined not to be captured by the myriad minorities whose utopian dreams he so powerfully projected. He presented himself as a devout Christian and a fierce public critic of Israel's occupation of Palestinian territory, yet he was also the first president to hold a seder in the White House. As newly elected chief executive, Obama sharply increased policing of America's border with Mexico and the prosecution and deportation of aliens with criminal records; only later in his term did he issue an executive order permanently blocking the deportation of 800,000 children of undocumented immigrants, most of whom were Latino and none of whom had been born in the United States. During his first campaign and for most of his first term, Obama rejected gay marriage and defended "Don't Ask, Don't Tell" in the military, only later ordering that gays and lesbians be allowed to participate openly in the Armed Forces and supporting gay marriage. The first African American president rarely spoke publicly about racism, the legacy of slavery, or the suffering of the black underclass, and he never proposed remedial governmental action aimed explicitly at this demographic group. Obama projected empathy for the powerless and excluded, but he did not present himself as serving them. He performed, rather, as a symbol of American democracy and on behalf of the wider, civil solidarity he believed it entailed.

The Demography of Democratic Solidarity

The hyphenated and polyglot history of the American nation means that every political campaign makes a point of speaking to different demographic groups. For the Obama campaign, the realities of the Electoral College – that presidential elections are won state-by-state rather than votes being aggregated nationally – made Latinos in the Southwest and Florida particularly important. Yet, when the president addressed this group, whether in person, in TV ads, or campaign material, he engaged in universalizing rhetoric, speaking a language of inclusion that placed its particular issues into the broadest possible frame: You can become part of the American whole, we respect you, we think your desires and needs are no different from those of other Americans. The home page of "Latinos for Obama" prominently displayed this presidential statement: "The stories of the Latino community are stories about the American Dream – young people who believe that anything is possible, and parents and grandparents working hard to give their children the chance to succeed." Rather than pandering – as in "Obama is a great friend of Latinos" – the Democratic campaign sought to bring Latinos under the wide umbrella of the civil sphere. Speaking in the midst of the campaign, in June 2012, to the annual conference of NALEO (National Association of Latino Elected and Appointed Officials), the president provided a clear example of this broad appeal, linking Latino group identity to the civil heart of the nation:

> We all have different backgrounds. We all have different political beliefs. The Latino community is not monolithic; the African American community is not all of one mind. This is a big country. And sometimes, in tough times, in a country this big and busy, especially during a political year, those differences are cast in a bright spotlight.

But I ran for this office because I am absolutely convinced that what binds us together has always proven stronger than what drives us apart. We are one people. We need one another. [Applause.] Our patriotism is rooted not in race, not in ethnicity, not in creed; it is based on a shared belief in the enduring and permanent promise of America.

That's the promise that draws so many talented, driven people to these shores. That's the promise that drew my own father here. That's the promise that drew your parents or grandparents or great grandparents – generations of people who dreamed of a place where knowledge and opportunity were available to anybody who was willing to work for it, anybody who was willing to seize it. A place where there was no limit to how far you could go, how high you could climb.

They took a chance. And America embraced their drive and embraced their courage – [and] said, "Come, you're welcome." This is who we are.[13]

In a video entitled "A special message for the Latino community," the president, this time speaking in Spanish, once again affirmed Latinos' connection to the wider American whole. The Latino community "lives up to the American Dream every day," Obama declared: "I'm running for a second term as president because I believe our country is strongest when those opportunities [for study and entrepreneurship] are within reach for everyone."[14] The official slogan for the Latino campaign, "Estamos unidos," suggested an unbroken union – "We are united."

Although Romney invested somewhat less in Spanish-language ads – $9.7 million on 8,500 ads compared to the Obama campaign's $12.4 million on 15,000 ads[15] – the most striking difference concerned quality not quantity. The Republicans emphasized Latino self-interest rather than their solidarity with the social whole. Their messages tended to focus on the economic sphere, addressing those who had suffered financially under Obama's tenure. And the overall tone was decidedly more negative, chastising the president rather than applauding Latinos' positive accomplishments and their contributions to the wider community. The Republican campaign put out an ad entitled, "Chavez for Obama," with clips of the widely reviled Venezuelan president and Mariela Castro – daughter of Cuban president Raul Castro and niece of Fidel – declaring they would vote for Obama.[16] Romney seemed to emphasize the particularistic, singling out his audience as "Hispanic Americans," and pointing out, "Hispanics are hurting."[17] He reiterated in several ads the higher unemployment and poverty rates among this community. The American Dream and widely shared democratic values were mentioned in only a handful of the Republicans' Spanish-language appeals.

The same kind of one-for-all-and-all-for-one theme framed Obama's appeals to other key demographic groups. In 2010, for example, he addressed the audience at an International Women's Day reception in just this way:

The story of America over the past 200 years – past 233 years is one of laws becoming more just, of a people becoming more equal, of a union being perfected. It's a story of captives being set free and a movement to fulfill the promise of that freedom. It's a story of waves of weary travelers reconsecrating America as a nation of immigrants. It's a story of our gay and lesbian brothers and sisters making the most of that most American of demands – to be treated the same as everybody else. And it's a story of women, from those on the Mayflower to the one I'm blessed to call my wife, who looked across the dinner table, and thought, I'm smarter than that guy. [Laughter.]

The story of women, along with gays and lesbians and immigrants, becomes a chapter in the larger national story of freedom, a brick in the arc of historical progress that builds the American dream.

The story of America's women, like the story of America itself, has had its peaks and valleys. But as one of our great American educators once said, if you drew a line through all the valleys and all the peaks, that line would be drawn with an upward curve. That upward curve – what we call progress – didn't happen by accident.[18]

Obama is suggesting that groups don't struggle only for themselves but also for others. In his 2012 commencement speech at Barnard, the president insisted that "what young generations have done before should give you hope."

Young folks who marched and mobilized and stood up and sat in, from Seneca Falls to Selma to Stonewall, didn't just do it for themselves; they did it for other people. [Applause.] That's how we achieved women's rights. That's how we achieved voting rights. That's how we achieved workers' rights. That's how we achieved gay rights. [Applause.] That's how we've made this Union more perfect. [Applause.][19]

At the 2012 LGBT pride reception hosted in the White House East Room, a yearly event of the Obama presidency, the group's struggles were linked to others that had come before:

Now, I've said before that I would never counsel patience; that it wasn't right to tell you to be patient any more than it was right for others to tell women to be patient a century ago, or African Americans to be patient a half century ago. After decades of inaction and indifference, you have every reason and right to push, loudly and forcefully, for equality.[20]

While the First Lady's campaign activities were most often addressed to families with children, when she spoke at a Black Caucus gala in 2012 she carefully folded the group's particular concerns into the universal dream of social solidarity:

This is the movement of our era – protecting that fundamental right [to vote] not just for this election, but for the next generation and generations to come. Because in the end, it's not just about who wins, or who loses, or who we vote for on Election Day. It's about who we are as Americans. It's about the democracy we want to leave for our kids and grandkids. It's about doing everything we can to carry on the legacy that is our inheritance not just as African Americans, but as Americans – as citizens of the greatest country on Earth.[21]

As the campaign heated up, such rhetoric connecting demography with democratic solidarity fused with talk about the campaign's singular historical significance, how the nation was balanced on the very hinge of history. The claim was advanced that a Romney victory would mean losing ground, pushing the country backwards, especially in ads targeted at women. The TV spot "Important" talked about contraception; it featured one woman saying, "This is not the 1950s," and another warning, "I think Romney would drag us back."[22] Portrayed as anti-civil, warnings about his backwardness were spiced with accusations of secrecy and duplicity. "Women need to know the real Mitt Romney,"[23] one ad declared, and another suggested "No matter what Mitt Romney's ads say, we know what he'll do."[24]

Revealingly, it was precisely Obama's *extra*-demographic symbolic stature – his performance of universalism and solidarity – that his conservative opponents so aggressively tried to undermine. Portraying him as a narrowly self-interested member of this or that marginalized and polluted minority, they claimed that Obama could not possibly represent traditional American values of the good and right. Such assertions often found a receptive audience on the right. Polls of Republican faithful variously reported that between 30 and 57 percent believed him to be a secret Muslim,[25] with nearly half (45 percent) asserting he had not been born in the United States, having forged his birth certificate so he could run for high public office.[26] In February, 2011, even as Obama was re-inflating his narrative and successfully placing himself at the center of the civil sphere, only 28 percent of Republicans professed to believe he was actually born in the United States.[27] Republican campaigners and support groups stoked these marginalizing efforts, and Mitt Romney was himself not immune to the mania. At an August campaign stop in Michigan, he joked: "I love being home, in this place where Ann and I were raised, where both of us were born ... No one's ever asked to see my birth certificate. They know that this is the place that we were born and raised."[28]

To challenge the claims that Obama's victory depended on demography is not to deny that the political culture of demographic groups made them more and less receptive to the Democrat's performance; nor is it to downplay the supercharged enthusiasm of activists who defined their identities in demographic terms – in particular, youth, single women, and Latinos. Members of demographic groups are active and reflective audiences, not passively defined by the color of their skin, their ethnic origins, gender, age, or sex. They select among the meanings projected to them by political performers, thinking and feeling about how they fit. It is the responses of such audiences, their affects and their cultural attentions, that allow meanings to be successfully extended from campaigning politicians to those whose votes they must win. Once again: Demography is not born but made.[29]

The active selecting and evaluating in which such "citizen-audiences" engage is what public opinion polls record. Not just polling, but every conceivable opinion-sorting technique is deployed by campaigns in their relentless search to find out what voters are thinking and what they might decide to do. The *Wall Street Journal* reported, with equal parts fascination and alarm, that "the Obama campaign has elevated poll-testing and focus-grouping to near-clinical heights, and the results drive the president's every action: his policies, his campaign venues, his targeted demographics, his messaging."[30] The *New York Times* wrote, with a mix of concern and admiration, about the Obama campaign's deployment of behavioral scientists to organize millions of bits of information into predictive models of where votes might lay.[31] While such reports were typically framed as Big Brother manipulation, it is possible to make exactly the opposite case. Such expensive efforts at intelligence gathering are rolled out because of the independent interpretive power of the citizen-audiences that political performers face, demographically demarcated audiences very much included.

Making Meaning with Social Media

In the age of social media, citizen-audiences become actors in more material ways. Beyond subjectively shifting their attention, changing the channel, telling the occasional pollster about their ideas, and talking to their friends, citizens now possess the virtual powers of political speech. They respond to political performances online, creating threads that become longer and sometimes more important than the stories triggering them. They create networks of communication by tweeting opinions and reactions, circles of virtual opinion that eventually expand into the public mainstream.

The fastest adopters of social media – young women, Hispanics, African Americans and Asian Americans[32] – were precisely the voting blocs that needed to be brought back into the fold after Obama's early symbolic deflation, fired up so they would vote, and motivated to become grass-roots organizers who could get their Democratic-leaning neighbors to polling places to cast their votes in similar ways. The symbolic connection that Obama was able to recreate with the American people in 2011, which intensified in 2012, expressed itself in social media. The massive increase in social media use among his supporters intensified this already-established connection between actor and audience, extending the campaign's cultural message, and increasing psychological identification in an emotional way.

In 2008, journalists and political opponents were dazzled by Obama's 2.3 million Facebook fans, which blossomed into 32.3 million by Election Day for 2012.[33] This time around, the techno-buzz was all about Twitter. In 2008, 1.8 million tweets were sent on Election Day; in 2012, 1.8 million tweets were sent every six minutes.[34] With more than 22 million followers, Obama far outpaced Romney, who had fewer than two million (1,760,388).[35] On election night, the Obama social media team broke the Twitter record for most retweeted post of all time, with a photo of the president hugging his wife and saying "four more years," garnering more than 350,000 retweets, and more than 122,000 favorites, by Election Day's end. And this tweet was just a fraction of the 31.7 million election-related tweets that day.[36] Overall, Obama dominated the online conversation, according to social media analysis firm Attention, taking up 64 percent in comparison with Romney's 34 percent.[37] As former Mean Street host Evan Newmark reminded Americans, however, a candidate needs charisma to use media effectively.[38] Quantity is nothing without quality. If political actors cannot fuse with their audience, there won't be tweets.

It is the sculpting of potentially sympathetic demographic groups into attentive, affected, and interpretive audiences, and the transformation of the latter into active agents via social media, that explains Obama's grass-roots campaign. To take weeks, months, and even years off from the routines of work, family, and school in order to go door-to-door, organize, and sometimes even live among communities at the grass roots requires extraordinary engagement. Such activists must be emotionally inspired by the candidate and feel symbolically connected to him. It is cultural connection, not demographic identity, that grows the grass roots. By the summer of 2012, the Obama campaign had 30,000 full-time volunteer organizers,[39] and 3,000 full-time paid organizers in the battleground states alone.[40] These activists could be sliced and diced demographically – as members of this or that demographic group. But their loyalties and convictions were not born but made: they were the most affected and committed core audience for Obama's long-playing political performance. The closing video of the 2012 campaign, the most viewed of all (more than 9 million times), recorded a drama of intense identification between political actor and the audience-turned-actor organizers of his national staff. Here is what the just re-elected president told a roomful of campaign staffers and volunteers in a surprise visit to Chicago headquarters the day after the election:

> When I come here and I look at all of you, what comes to mind – it's not that you guys actually remind me of myself. It's the fact that you are so much better than I was in so many ways. You're smarter and better organized and you're more effective. So I'm absolutely confident that all of you are going to do just amazing things in your lives. And what Bobby Kennedy calls the ripples of hope that come out when you throw a stone in a lake – that's going to be you.

As the triumphant politician continued speaking to his rapt audience about how they would all go out and be successful in whatever they worked at, he teared up, barely choking out, "I'm really proud of all of you."[41]

The job of these dedicated organizers was to connect with *their* audiences in turn – the potential voters. All the grass-roots cultural work of performing, messaging, and receiving – all this symbolic fusion – was not an end in itself. The point was extending this energy so it would bring out the vote.[42] This effort succeeded. The 2.2 million volunteers working out of

813 field offices[43] were part of a mobilizing effort that combined highly advanced data crunching with the old-fashioned personal touch or, as campaign manager Jim Messina put it, the numerical and the human.[44] And it was the latter than mattered most. All the "analytics" produced by the campaign's behavioral research were aimed simply at making face-to-face connections more frequent and fulfilling.[45] In a *Huffington Post* piece entitled "It's the Relationship, Stupid," Robert Hall argued "the game-changer was the Obama campaign's capability to systematically build local, personal relationships that translated into votes."[46] According to a memo issued by the campaign in early November, 125,646,479 human contacts – phone calls or visits – had been made. Automated robo-calls or leaving literature at the door were not included. This figure (over two-and-a-half times the number for the Romney campaign) translated into one human contact for every 2.5 people in the country.[47]

The gold standard of such human campaigning occurred between people who actually knew each other. According to Yale researchers, "in-person canvassing raised turnout from around 44 percent to 53 percent, but being contacted by someone you know raised response rates four times."[48] In the final weeks leading up to the election, the Obama campaign took neighborhood door-knocking to a new virtual height. Through a Facebook application geared at "targeted sharing," one million users let the campaign into their private world, allowing access to their friend lists. With the click of a button, more than 600,000 of these supporters contacted their more than 5 million friends, asking them variously to register to vote, to give money, and to vote – or to look at a video designed to change their mind. *TIME Magazine* reported that early tests of the system found "statistically significant changes in voter behavior."[49] Describing this unprecedented social media reach-out, the campaign's digital director suggested it had transformed audiences into actors and friends into audiences. "People don't trust campaigns. They don't even trust media organizations. Who do they trust? Their friends."[50] Even the most remote Obama-for-America offices were in daily digital contact with their state organizing offices. What these electrical impulses carried was cultural content. A continuous stream of images, speeches, and morale-building messages from the president and his inner staff were tweeted and emailed day and night. When organizers went door to door to expand these projections personally, they were instructed to send their results homeward digitally after every visit. Those with an iPhone could use an application to immediately report which one of seven categories a person answering the door fit into, from "Strong Obama" to "Strong Republican" or "Not Voting."[51]

The Obama ground game was a play-within-the-play, a powerfully choreographed, face-to-face performance that unfolded inside the broader performance of the election campaign. Its success depended upon the rhetorical performances carried over the airwaves being successful, and its actor-organizers were chosen from those most affected by it. It was Romney's failure over the airwaves – his difficulties connecting with core Republican audiences – that made it impossible for his campaign to sustain a ground game strong enough to get out critical votes.

The Democrats' culturally networked ground game – fueled by Obama's performances over the airwaves – worked its magic on Election Day. In the battleground states targeted, the ground game may have raised voter turnout by an estimated 1–3 percent.[52] In some states, this provided extra padding. In a few others, it may have made the difference between victory and defeat. In Ohio, the campaign elevated the African American share of the electorate from 11 percent on 2008 to 15 percent, translating into more than 200,000 new votes in a state decided by a margin of 165,000.[53]

Making Meaning with Money

All this took money, lots of it. Hundreds of field offices, thousands of paid staff, ad makers and poll takers, television time, and social media facilities – none of this happens for free. Both the Obama and the Romney campaigns raised over a billion dollars in 2012 ($1.123 billion and $1.019 billion respectively).[54] Social scientists, along with political pundits, are inclined to believe that money talks, that he who pays the piper calls the tune. In democratic politics, the reverse is more often the case. Money talks, but it also listens, and what it hears usually decides who and how much will be paid. The piper chooses the tune. If it's melodious, those with money come forward; if harsh and dissonant, they keep their hands in their pockets and stay away.[55]

Contemplating the challenge of funding his last campaign, observers believed Obama to be severely disadvantaged. The first strike against him was unlimited corporate money. In January, 2010, the Supreme Court declared political spending protected speech under the First Amendment, preventing government from putting limits on corporate campaign donations. Pundits made dire predictions about the effect of the "Citizens United" decision on democratic politics. In an October, 2010 editorial, "Money Talks Louder Than Ever in Midterm Elections," the New York Times reported that outside spending had more than doubled compared with the same point in the 2006 election, and "overwhelming favored Republicans."[56] The second strike against the president was his alienation of Wall Street. The stock marketers and investment bankers who had invested in Obama in 2008 apparently felt they had received less than nothing in return. In 2012, facing what they regarded as massive new regulatory legislation, Wall Street placed its bets on Romney, the Republican businessman politician who promised to eliminate taxes and red tape.

Obama's financial prospects looked bleak.[57] There are two reasons why they didn't turn out to be. One is that, in democratic politics, money is means, not end. Material resources are needed, but only as facilitation, to allow performances to get on stage. Gaining access to the stage enables performance, but it cannot control its content or reception. You can buy talent, but you can't make it play. Most Hollywood films, Broadway shows, and advertising campaigns fail, no matter how lavish their investments. In 2012, Republicans had huge sums at their disposal, but the ads they bought, the staff they hired, the candidate that emerged – none was able to fuse with citizen-audiences in broad and powerful ways.[58] In fact, on a democratic playing field, big money can be a symbolic disadvantage. Romney's personal wealth and his ties to the corporate world were potentially polluting. "Citizens United" allowed large sums to be secretly donated. But, while legal, the question remained whether such funding would be dramatically effective. Money can easily be made to seem anti-civil, and for large amounts of secret money, this is almost a sure thing.

The other reason Democratic funding worries proved groundless had to do with the elasticity of political donations. At the middle and upper levels, individuals, occupational groups, and economic classes have more money than they spend on daily needs. Such discretionary funds are available if they feel "called" to give. When Obama regained his symbolic footing in 2011, he was able to "call" audiences in this way. Wealthy donors from previous years felt reconnected. Making political contributions is yet another way that sitting audiences can stand up and become actors. And in addition to writing checks, many of the affluent became organizational actors themselves. As "bundlers," they actively reached out to others in their occupation and class. Among the less affluent, social media solicitations allowed them to become active donors on a smaller scale. Yes, there was less money from Wall Street. Goldman Sachs had been the number one donor for Obama's 2008 campaign, but the firm switched to Romney and the Republicans for 2012.[59] But Main Street stepped up its investment for Obama's last campaign. Unlike Romney's supporters among the titans of the financial world – Goldman Sachs, Bank of America, Morgan Stanley, JP Morgan Chase & Co., and Wells Fargo – the top contributors to the Obama campaign included universities, Microsoft and Google, the entertainment industry, and the US government.[60]

Conclusion

In these final remarks, we return to our chosen instrument of political analysis – the microscope of close reading and granular observation rather than the telescope, with its long view and distant observation. Instead of searching for deep underlying causes of the Democratic victory, we have focused on the moment-to-moment concatenations of the actual campaign, the ordinary speech acts, the dramas on stump and advertisement and the commentaries about them, by journalists, pundits, and bloggers, in newspaper, television, and blogs. We have examined the fine thread that stretches between political actors and their audiences, demonstrating how hard each of these sides works to be understood and how difficult it is to bring them together, and at the craft and the cunning and just plain dumb luck that is necessary for political performances to be successful and broadly inspiring in the present day.

During Barack Obama's first term and his last campaign, the president and his opponents confronted huge issues – economic lurches, demographic shifts, polarizing ideologies, global tides. But if we want to understand the outcomes of electoral struggles, such grand issues do not cut close enough to the bone. They were not the cause of Obama's political recovery, his subsequent electoral victory, or Romney's defeat. How the big issues were dramatized is what mattered. It was about form, poise, narrative, and timing, about keeping your own side pure while dusting up your opponent's, making your own team sacred and the other profane.

We have not been interested in big structures but in minute processes. Not in the why but the how.

If Obama's performances had not been so dramatically effective – during the second half of his first term and during his last campaign – minorities would not have voted for the Democrats in such high numbers, and his share of white voters would have fallen. Obama's grass-roots team would have been much more difficult to mobilize. The symbolic deflation that almost destroyed his presidency during the first years of his term, rather than being reversed, would have deepened, with mortal effects on his re-election bid. After the midterm debacle of November, 2010, there would have been no re-inflation. The media would have continued to be dismissive, and his support among liberal elites would have continued to melt away. If Obama had not symbolized so effectively in 2011 – in the face of a hostile right-wing House of Representatives and a myriad of other challenging contingencies – Romney would have appeared a better man in 2012, especially in the light of an economy which would have been much more widely construed as failing.

After the Democrats' ignominious defeat in November, 2010, pundits, statisticians, political scientists, and journalists asserted that the odds were stacked against President Obama's re-election, and predicted his demise. The incumbent faced the stiffest economic headwinds in 70 years, and an historic Supreme Court decision had thrown open the corporate spending gates. Besides, he was black, a demographic factor that would drive white support down so far it would guarantee electoral defeat. None of these predictions turned out to be correct.

It is the performance of politics that determines the fate of political campaigns. Who can grasp the nettle of the collective consciousness? Who can write scripts fitting the great themes of national history to the particular challenges of this time and place? Who can persuade citizens that their election will bring national salvation, or at least prevent a terrible fall from grace? Who can become a compelling symbol of democratic hopes and dreams, sculpting a political image that embodies freedom and solidarity in a wise and worldly way? Whoever makes meaning better will be the victor in a presidential campaign.

Obama Power offers a new interpretation of US politics in the critical four years from January 2009 to November 2012 – and perhaps beyond.

Notes

Introduction

1 This book is not written for academics, but it is not written against them, either. Our play-by-play analysis of the drama-rich, thickly textured, punch-by-punch struggles of Obama's first term and his last campaign rests upon some deeply imbedded social theories. Readers of *Obama Power* don't necessarily need to know about this stuff, but they might be interested anyway. If so, they could look at some of the following: Jeffrey C. Alexander, *The Meanings of Social Life: A Cultural Sociology* (New York: Oxford, 2003), *The Civil Sphere* (New York: Oxford, 2006), *Performance and Power* (London and New York: Polity, 2011), and Jeffrey C. Alexander, Ronald N. Jacobs, and Philip Smith, eds., *The Oxford Handbook of Cultural Sociology* (New York: Oxford University Press, 2012).

Chapter 1   The Performance of Politics

1 Maureen Dowd, "Can the Dude Abide?" *New York Times*, October 30, 2010, accessed July 4, 2013 from http://www.nytimes.com/2010/10/31/opinion/31dowd.html?_r=0.
2 Alan Fram, "College Students' Obamamania Wanes: AP-mtvU Poll," *HuffPost College*, October 13, 2010, accessed July 4, 2013 from http://www.huffingtonpost.com/2010/10/13/college-students-obamaman_n_761410.html.
3 Hollie McKay, "Liberal Hollywood Quiet for 2010 Midterm Elections, Experts Say," *FOX News*, October 26, 2010, accessed July 4, 2013 from http://www.foxnews.com/entertainment/2010/10/26/hollywood-celebrities-vote-elections-midterms-enthusiasm-gap/.

4 Peter Baker, "In Republican Victories, Tide Turns Starkly," *New York Times*, November 2, 2010, accessed July 4, 2013 from http://www.nytimes.com/2010/11/03/us/politics/03assess.html.

5 Louise Radnofsky and Michael M. Phillips, "As US Political Divide Widened, a Friendship Fell Into the Rift," *Wall Street Journal*, November 9, 2010, accessed July 4, 2013 from http://online.wsj.com/article/SB10001424052748704805204575595231978784218.html.

6 James Taranto, "The Empire Strikes Back; The GOP picks up six Senate seats. Let the recriminations begin!" *Wall Street Journal*, November 4, 2010, accessed July 4, 2013 from http://online.wsj.com/article/SB10001424052748703805704575594430240937908.html.

7 Byron York, "Obama, New GOP Lawmakers Are on Collision Course," *Townhall.com*, November 9, 2010, accessed July 4, 2013 from http://townhall.com/columnists/byronyork/2010/11/09/obama,_new_gop_lawmakers_are_on_collision_course/page/full/.

8 Hendrik Hertzberg, "Electoral Dissonance," *New Yorker*, November 9, 2010, accessed July 4, 2013 from http://www.newyorker.com/talk/comment/2010/11/15/101115taco_talk_hertzberg.

9 Michael Scherer, "Tea Party Time: The Making of a Political Uprising," *TIME Magazine*, September 16, 2010, accessed July 4, 2013 from http://www.time.com/time/magazine/article/0,9171,2019608,00.html.

10 "Republican Post-Midterm Elections Agenda," *C-SPAN Video Library*, November 3, 2010, accessed July 4, 2013 from http://www.c-spanvideo.org/program/296405-1.

11 Marl Leibovich and Ashley Parker, "Tea Partiers and Republican Faithful Share Exuberant Celebrations," *New York Times*, November 3, 2010, accessed July 4, 2013 from http://www.nytimes.com/2010/11/03/us/politics/03scene.html.

12 Peter Baker, "In Republican Victories, Tide Turns Starkly."

13 Karl Rove, "From Post-Partisan to Most Partisan. President Obama has energized his opponents by demonizing them," *Wall Street Journal*, December 16, 2010, accessed July 4, 2013 from http://online.wsj.com/article/SB1000142405274870482810457602163105912628.html.

14 "Tearful Boehner says 'not a time for celebration'; Rep. John Boehner, R-Ohio, on track to become the next House speaker, addressed the Republican election victories in an emotional speech," *NBC News*, November 3, 2010, accessed July 4, 2013 from http://www.nbcnews.com/video/nbc-news/39980261#39980261.

15 "Factbox: What they're saying about the midterm elections," *Reuters*, November 3, 2010, accessed July 4, 2013 from http:// www.reuters.com/article/2010/11/03/us-usa-elections-quotes-idUS TRE6A20QP20101103.

16 "The Liberal Reckoning of 2010; The year voters saw the left's unvarnished agenda and said no," *Wall Street Journal*, January 3, 2011, accessed July 4, 2013 from http://online.wsj.com/article/SB10 001424052748703909904576051803529108190.html.

17 Peter Baker, "In Republican Victories, Tide Turns Starkly." The *Wall Street Journal* reported: "Nearly one in three voters, 32%, said they would use their midterm vote as a way to send a message of opposition to President Barack Obama, while 27% said they would vote to send a message of support for the president. A plurality, 39%, said Obama would have nothing to do with how they cast their vote" (Susan Davis, "WSJ/NBC Poll: Voters Support GOP Takeover of Congress," *Wall Street Journal* (*Washington Wire*), June 23, 2010, accessed July 4, 2013 from http://blogs.wsj.com/washwire/2010/06/23/wsjnbc-poll-gop-controlled-congress-gains-support/).

18 For a graphic representation of polling data from Gallup that measured the dramatic fall-off of interest in the 2010 election among blacks, youth, and non-Hispanic whites, see Lydia Saad, "Blacks, Young Voters Not Poised for High Turnout on Nov. 2; Republicans – and conservative Republicans in particular – are already tuned in to midterms," *Gallup Politics*, September 3, 2010, accessed June 23, 2013 from http://www.gallup.com/poll/142877/ blacks-young-voters-not-poised-high-turnout-nov.aspx. For poll data on what the *New York Times*' Nate Silver called the "enthusiasm gap," see "Understanding and Misunderstanding the 'Enthusiasm Gap,'" *New York Times* (*FiveThirtyEight*), October 6, 2010, accessed June 23, 2013 from http://fivethirtyeight.blogs.nytimes.com/20 10/10/06/understanding-and-misunderstanding-the-enthusiasm-gap/.

19 Katie Couric, "Will Young Voters Ditch the Midterms?" *CBS Evening News*, October 22, 2010, accessed July 4, 2013 from http:// www.cbsnews.com/stories/2010/10/21/eveningnews/main6979648. shtml.

20 Perry Bacon, Jr., "Low turnout by young voters hurts Democrats in midterm elections," *Washington Post*, November 3, 2010, accessed July 4, 2013 from http://www.washingtonpost.com/wp-dyn/content/ article/2010/11/03/AR2010110304486.html.

21 Lydia Saad, "Blacks, Young Voters Not Poised for High Turnout on Nov. 2."

22 Kevin Sack, "Black Turnout Will Be Crucial for Democrats," *New*

York Times, October 16, 2010, accessed July 4, 2013 from http://www.nytimes.com/2010/10/17/us/politics/17blackvote.html.

23 Kate Zernike, "Democrats Need a Rally Monkey," *New York Times*, March 6, 2010, accessed July 4, 2013 from http://www.nytimes.com/2010/03/07/weekinreview/07zernike.html.

24 Lydia Saad, "Americans Believe GOP Should Consider Tea Party Ideas: Half of Republicans are Tea Party supporters; 5% are 'opponents'," *Gallup Politics*, January 31, 2011, accessed July 4, 2013 from http://www.gallup.com/poll/145838/americans-believe-gop-consider-tea-party-ideas.aspx.

25 Elizabeth Drew, "In the Bitter New Washington," *New York Review of Books*, December 23, 2010, accessed July 4, 2013 from http://www.nybooks.com/articles/archives/2010/dec/23/bitter-new-washington/.

26 Peter Baker, "Obama Says the G.O.P. is Beholden to Interests," *New York Times*, October 11, 2010, accessed June 23, 2013 from http://query.nytimes.com/gst/fullpage.html?res=9401E5DA143FF932A25753C1A9669D8B63.

27 Peter Baker, "Obama Strains to Get Liberals Back Into Fold Ahead of Vote," *New York Times*, October 5, 2010, accessed June 23, 2013 from http://www.nytimes.com/2010/10/06/us/politics/06obama.html.

28 The kind of evidence we will marshal for this claim broadly resembles the range of data we have cited in the present chapter. We thoroughly sample quotes and observations from cable and network television news, weekly news and political magazines, regional newspapers, national and international press services, blogs, YouTube, and polling organizations. At the same time, we rely more heavily than any other source on national news stories published in the *New York Times* and the *Wall Street Journal*. Quotations reported by these two national newspapers, and their journalistic interpretations of ongoing political events, constitute about one-third of the references in this book. No matter how Americans receive the news, whether from newspapers, television, radio, or blogs, the most influential national news decisions – about which events are deemed to be newsworthy and how they are interpreted – are made by the reporters and editors of the *Times* and the *Journal* and, though less frequently, the *Washington Post*. Moreover, while the editorial page writings of the *Times* are to the left and the *Journal* to the right, in terms of news reporting – the selection and interpretation of political "facts" – they rarely disagree. There is significant social-scientific support for this overrepresentation of these national newspapers. On the central role of the *New York Times* in agenda-setting, for example, see Fiona

Clark and Deborah L. Illman, "Content Analysis of *New York Times* Coverage of Space Issues for the Year 2000," *Science Communication* 25(3) (2003): 24; Stephen J. Farnsworth and S. Robert Lichter, "The Mediated Congress: Coverage of Capitol Hill in the *New York Times* and the *Washington Post*," *Harvard International Journal of Press/Politics* 10 (2005): 94; and William L. Benoit, Kevin A. Stein, and Glenn J. Hansen, "*New York Times* Coverage of Presidential Campaigns," *Journalism and Mass Communication Quarterly* 82(2) (2005): 360. On the relative insignificance for news reporting of the editorial leanings of the *Times* and the *Journal*, see Reed Irvine and Cliff Kincaid, "Post Columnist Concerned about Media Bias," *Media Monitor (Accuracy in Media)*, September 17, 2007, accessed September 20, 2013 from http://www.aim.org/media-monitor/post-columnist-concerned-about-media-bias/; Paul Sperry, "Myth of the Conservative Wall Street Journal," *WorldNetDaily*, June 25, 2002, accessed September 20, 2013 from http://www.wnd.com/index.php?pageId=14357; and Daniel E. Ho and Kevin M. Quinn, "Measuring Explicit Political Positions of Media," *Quarterly Journal of Political Science* 3 (2008): 363. This largely consensual constitution of news establishes a foundation of "political facts" for other national and regional forums, including more polarized cable outlets such as MSNBC and Fox News, whose representations of politics speak to already committed, core political constituencies in ideologically explicit ways. During the first term of Obama's presidency, MSNBC moved considerably to the left, becoming what the *New York Times* called the "anti-Fox" and displacing CNN in the cable news ratings (Brian Stelter, "The Anti-Fox Gains Ground," *New York Times*, November 11, 2012, accessed June 24, 2013 from http://www.nytimes.com/2012/11/12/business/media/msnbc-its-ratings-rising-gains-ground-on-fox-news.html). The sources that constitute the other two-thirds of our references – our main sources in addition to the *Times* and the *Journal* – are widely distributed and broadly representative. They include YouTube, WhiteHouse.gov, FiveThirtyEight, the Princeton Election Consortium, the Gallup Organization, the Pew Research Center, the Huffington Post, the three major network news outlets, Fox News, MSNBC, CNN.com, Politico, MichelleMalkin. com, Red State, Talking Points Memo, The Blaze, *People Magazine*, *TIME Magazine*, the *New Yorker*, the *New Republic*, *Newsweek*, *USA Today*, and the *Washington Post*.

The challenge for a political sociology focusing on cultural texts and their performances is to demonstrate that such campaign rhetoric and the commentary of media pundits actually has an effect on voters. How does one know that ordinary voters – as distinct from,

say, East Coast elites – were listening to what was being said by
political actors and reported and opined by journalists and pundits
in the *New York Times,* the *Washington Post,* and the *Wall Street
Journal?* In the pages that follow, we are closely attuned to this
problem, which we think of as the "performance-audience" issue.
What distinguishes our approach from a more purely textually ori-
ented cultural sociology – one that focuses on only elite speakers
and writers – is our separation of audiences from actors. With such
a separation, the empirical problem becomes how and if the two
become connected. We are interested, therefore, not only in inter-
preting the nature of cultural messages but also in how they are
received by audiences. It is for this reason that we continuously inter-
weave poll results with our interpretations of political performances
("texts"). Honoring the critical capacities of "the masses" means to
understand citizens as actively judging audiences. Often, but by no
means always, segmented into conservative, liberal, and centrist sections of the national political theater, these "citizen-audiences" have
the capacity to respond differently, depending on the performance's
aesthetic and moral qualities. Polls provide the most statistically representative evidence of how the masses of voters are being affected
by, and are responsive to, the cultural messages projected by political
actors, demonstrating that such responses are not limited to the elites
who read the *Post,* the *Journal,* and the *Times.* We amplify these
polling data with a multitude of other kinds of evidence: televised
nightly news programs, which are the most widely attended to public
projections of political performance; influential and ideologically
diverse political blogs; social media; publicly available government
sources; and widely reported remarks by "ordinary people." As we
explain further in our concluding chapter, it is primarily through
public opinion polls, blogs, and social media that citizens at the
receiving end of political messages make themselves heard. They do
this in a big way, creating a real back and forth between elite performances and mass public opinion. It is because of the existence of this
dialectic that we continuously observe elite performers trying to take
into account mass reaction in the course of their public actions, as
they anticipate audience responses. In this manner, audiences become
political actors themselves.

Chapter 2   Symbolic Deflation

1 Ian Urbina, "Beyond Beltway, Health Debate Turns Hostile," *New
York Times,* August 7, 2009, accessed July 4, 2013 from http://www.
nytimes.com/2009/08/08/us/politics/08townhall.html.

Some Democratic members opted for "tele-town halls," through conference calls, rather than having face-to-face meetings.

2 "Tea Party Express Takes Washington By Storm," *Fox News*, September 12, 2009, accessed July 4, 2013 from http://www.foxnews.com/politics/2009/09/12/tea-party-express-takes-washington-storm/.

3 Even after the Act was passed on March 23, 2010, and upheld by the Supreme Court two years later, the movement, although diminished, has continued, pushing to repeal or hamstring it. This resistance gained some force with the faltering roll-out of the Act in Fall 2013.

4 An April 2010 poll revealed that 92 percent of Tea Party supporters believed Obama was "moving the country toward socialism," a sentiment shared by more than half of the general public (Kate Zernike and Megan Thee-Brenan, "Poll Finds Tea Party Backers Wealthier and More Educated," *New York Times*, April 14, 2010, accessed July 4, 2013 from http://www.nytimes.com/2010/04/15/us/politics/15poll.html).

5 David A. Patten, "Armey, Tea Party Patriots Plan 'Die-In' and More Protests," *Newsmax*, December 14, 2009, accessed July 4, 2013 from http://www.newsmax.com/Headline/tea-party-patriots-healthcare/2009/12/14/id/342614#ixzz2PJQc9UZx.

6 "Health Care," *Tea Party Patriots*, n.d., accessed July 4, 2013 from http://www.teapartypatriots.org/resources/health/.

7 Evan Thomas, "The Case for Killing Granny," *Newsweek Magazine*, September 11, 2009, accessed July 4, 2013 from http://www.thedailybeast.com/newsweek/2009/09/11/the-case-for-killing-granny.html.

8 Rachel Weiner, "Palin: Obama's 'Death Panel' Could Kill My Down Syndrome Baby," *HuffPost Politics*, September 7, 2009, accessed July 4, 2013 from http://www.huffingtonpost.com/2009/08/07/palin-obamas-death-panel_n_254399.html.

9 Elise Viebeck, "Poll: Four in 10 believe in Obama healthcare law 'death panels,'" *The Hill*, September 26, 2012, accessed July 4, 2013 from http://thehill.com/blogs/healthwatch/health-reform-implementation/258753-poll-four-in-10-believe-in-health-law-death-panels.

10 WSJ Staff, "Transcript of President Obama's Town Hall Meeting on Health Care," *Wall Street Journal* (*Washington Wire*), August 15, 2009, accessed July 14, 2013 from http://blogs.wsj.com/washwire/2009/08/15/transcript-of-president-obamas-town-hall-meeting-on-health-care/.

11 Byron Williams, "Isn't Adequate Healthcare a Moral Issue?" *Huffington Post*, September 6, 2009, accessed July 4, 2013 from http://

www.huffingtonpost.com/byron-williams/isnt-adequate-health care_b_278434.html.

12 Mary Lu Carnevale, "Prepared Text of Obama's Speech on Health Care," *Wall Street Journal* (*Washington Wire*), September 9, 2009, accessed July 4, 2013 from http://blogs.wsj.com/washwire/2009/09/09/prepared-text-of-obamas-speech-on-health-care/.

13 Kevin Sack and Marjorie Connelly, "In Poll, Wide Support for Government-Run Health," *New York Times*, June 20, 2009, accessed July 4, 2013 from http://www.nytimes.com/2009/06/21/health/policy/21poll.html?_r=0.

14 Sarah Dutton, Jennifer De Pinto, Fred Backus, and Anthony Salvanto, "Poll: 47% disapprove of Obama health care law," *CBS News*, March 26, 2012, accessed July 4, 2013 from http://www.cbsnews.com/8301-503544_162-57404342-503544/poll-47-disapprove-of-obama-health-care-law/.

15 Jill Smolowe, with Sandra Sobieraj Westfall, Sharon Cotliar, Tiffany McGee, Nina Burleigh, Mary Green, Arnesa Howell, and Wendy Grossman, "We Have Chosen Hope," *People*, February 2, 2009, Vol. 71, No. 4, accessed September 20, 2013 from http://www.people.com/people/archive/article/0,,20258302,00.html.

16 "Election Will Turn on These Key Economic Issues," *Wall Street Journal Live*, July 24, 2012, accessed July 4, 2013 from http://live.wsj.com/video/election-will-turn-on-these-key-economic-issues/E94792C1-D39D-4F93-8335-688CCBA37FD7.html.

17 Brian Montopoli, "Transcript: Obama Remarks At Stimulus Signing," *CBS News*, February 17, 2009, accessed July 4, 2013 from http://www.cbsnews.com/8301-503544_162-4807704-503544.html.

18 "Labor Force Statistics from the Current Population Survey, 2003–2013," *Bureau of Labor Statistics*, n.d., accessed July 4, 2013 from http://data.bls.gov/timeseries/LNS14000000.

19 Pamela Warrick, "Heeeeeeere's Barack Obama!" *People.com*, March 19, 2009, accessed July 4, 2013 from http://www.people.com/people/article/0,,20266884,00.html.

20 John Harwood, "But Can Obama Make the Trains Run on Time?" *New York Times* (*The Caucus*), April 19, 2009, accessed July 4, 2013 from http://www.nytimes.com/2009/04/20/us/politics/20caucus.html.

21 Michelle Malkin, "Barack Obama's savior-based economy," *Michelle Malkin*, February 11, 2009, accessed July 4, 2013 from http://michellemalkin.com/2009/02/11/barack-obamas-savior-based-economy/.

22 Brad Heath, "Poll: 57% don't see stimulus working," *USA Today*,

August 17, 2009, accessed July 4, 2013 from http://usatoday30.usa-today.com/money/economy/2009-08-16-stimulus-poll_N.htm.

23 John D. McKinnon, "Public Opinion on Key Obama Policies Sinks," *Wall Street Journal* (*Washington Wire*), November 3, 2009, accessed July 4, 2013 from http://blogs.wsj.com/washwire/2009/11/03/public-opinion-sinks-on-key-obama-policies/. CBS News polling reported an even lower approval rating on the economy, 38 percent in mid-October (Sarah Dutton, "Obama's Approval Rating on Economy Just 38 Percent – But it Could be Worse," *CBS News Polls*, October 18, 2010, accessed July 4, 2013 from http://www.cbsnews.com/8301-503544_162-20019953-503544.html).

24 Larry Hackett, "An Exclusive Interview with the Obamas Our First Year," *People*, January 25, 2010, Vol. 73, No. 3, accessed July 4, 2013 from http://www.people.com/people/archive/article/0,,20342928,00.html.

25 Jonathan Weisman, "Gloom Spreads on Economy, but GOP Doesn't Gain," *Wall Street Journal*, October 29, 2009, accessed July 4, 2013 from http://online.wsj.com/article/SB125667589615011225.html.

26 Larry Hackett, "An Exclusive Interview with the Obamas."

27 Jonathan Chait, "What the Left Doesn't Understand About Obama," *New York Times Magazine*, September 2, 2011, accessed July 4, 2013 from http://www.nytimes.com/2011/09/04/magazine/what-the-left-doesnt-understand-about-obama.html?ref=magazine&_r=0.

28 David Brooks, "The Tea Party Teens," *New York Times*, January 4, 2010, accessed July 4, 2013 from http://www.nytimes.com/2010/01/05/opinion/05brooks.html?_r=0.

29 "Presidential Remarks at Senate Rally for Martha Coakley," *C-SPAN Video Library*, January 17, 2010, accessed July 4, 2013 from http://www.c-spanvideo.org/program/291410-2.

30 Michelle Malkin, "Massachusetts Miracle: Election night liveblog; Update: BROWN WINS, COAKLEY CONCEDES; Brown victory speech cheers: '41!41!41!'" *Michelle Malkin*, January 19, 2010, accessed July 4, 2013 from http://michellemalkin.com/2010/01/19/massachusetts-miracle-election-night-liveblog/.

31 Josh Marshall, "Good Attitude, Russ!" *Talking Points Memo*, January 19, 2010, accessed July 4, 2013 from http://www.talkingpointsmemo.com/archives/2010/01/good_attitude_russ.php.

32 Josh Marshall, "Good Attitude, Russ!"

33 Susan Davis, "Scott Brown Wins in Massachusetts: A Reaction Round-Up," *Wall Street Journal* (*Washington Wire*), January 19, 2010, accessed July 4, 2013 from http://blogs.wsj.com/washwire/2010/01/19/scott-brown-wins-in-massachusetts-a-reaction-round-up/.

34 Adam Nagourney, Jeff Zeleny, Kate Zernike, and Michael Cooper, "G.O.P. Used Energy and Stealth to Win Seat," *New York Times*, January 20, 2010, accessed July 4, 2013 from http://www.nytimes. com/2010/01/21/us/politics/21reconstruct.html.
35 Karen Travers, "Exclusive: President Obama: We Lost Touch with American People Last Year," *ABC News*, January 20, 2010, accessed July 4, 2013 from http://abcnews.go.com/WN/Politics/pres ident-obama-lost-touch-american-people-year/story?id=9613462#. UYELncodhEI.
36 Vanessa Williamson, Theda Skocpol, and John Coggin, "The Tea Party and the Remaking of Republican Conservatism," *Perspectives on Politics*, 9(1) (2011): 32, accessed July 4, 2013 from http://scholar. harvard.edu/files/williamson/files/tea_party_pop.pdf.
37 Adam Nagourney, et al., "G.O.P. Used Energy and Stealth to Win Seat."
38 The Editors, "Tea Partyers and the Power of No," *New York Times*, January 31, 2010, accessed July 4, 2013 from http://roomfordebate. blogs.nytimes.com/2010/01/31/tea-partyers-and-the-power-of-no/.
39 "Study #10049 NBC News/*Wall Street Journal* Survey January 23-25, 2010," *MSNBC*, n.d., accessed July 4, 2013 from http://msn-bcmedia.msn.com/i/MSNBC/Sections/NEWS/A_Politics/__Politics_ Today_Stories_Teases/10049NBCWSJ.pdf.
40 Kate Zernike, "Notes From the Tea Party Convention," *New York Times (The Caucus)*, February 6, 2010, accessed July 4, 2013 from http://thecaucus.blogs.nytimes.com/2010/02/06/notes-from-the-tea-party-convention/.
41 Helen Cooper, "Obama: A Giant-Killer, Feeling His Oats," *New York Times*, March 27, 2010, accessed July 4, 2013 from http:// www.nytimes.com/2010/03/28/weekinreview/28cooper.html.
42 Charles M. Blow, "Could Obama Be Invincible?" *New York Times*, March 19, 2010, accessed July 4, 2013 from http://www.nytimes. com/2010/03/20/opinion/20blow.html.
43 Frank Rich, "It's a Bird, It's a Plane, It's Obama!" *New York Times*, April 3, 2010, accessed July 4, 2013 from http://www.nytimes. com/2010/04/04/opinion/04rich.html.
44 Jesse Lee, "This is What Change Looks Like," *The White House Blog*, March 22, 2010, accessed July 4, 2013 from http://www.white house.gov/blog/2010/03/22/what-change-looks.
45 Sarah Dutton, et al., "Poll: 47% disapprove of Obama health care law."
46 Charles M. Blow, "An Article of Faith," *New York Times*, April 2, 2010, accessed June 23, 2013 from http://www.nytimes.com/ 2010/04/03/opinion/03blow.html.

47 Maureen Dowd, "A Storyteller Loses the Story Line," *New York Times*, June 1, 2010, accessed June 23, 2013 from http://www.nytimes.com/2010/06/02/opinion/02dowd.html.

48 Frank Newport, "Obama Receives 44% Approval on Oil Spill While BP Gets 16%: Obama's overall job approval rating, at 47% last week, is little changed," *Gallup Politics*, June 21, 2010, accessed July 4, 2013 from http://www.gallup.com/poll/140957/obama-receives-approval-oil-spill-gets.aspx.

49 Charles M. Blow, "The Thrill Is Gone," *New York Times*, June 18, 2010, accessed July 4, 2013 from http://www.nytimes.com/2010/06/19/opinion/19blow.html.

50 Michael Scherer, "How Barack Obama Became Mr. Unpopular," *TIME Magazine*, September 3, 2010, accessed July 4, 2013 from http://www.time.com/time/magazine/article/0,9171,2015779,00.html.

51 "Waiting for Mr. Obama," *New York Times*, August 28, 2010, accessed July 4, 2013 from http://www.nytimes.com/2010/08/29/opinion/29sun1.html.

52 "President Barack Obama on 'The View' (Live-Blog)," *Wall Street Journal* (*Speakeasy*), July 29, 2010, accessed July 4, 2013 from http://blogs.wsj.com/speakeasy/2010/07/29/president-barack-obama-on-the-view-live-blog/.

53 Chris Stirewalt, "Fox News Polls Track Tea Party Influence in 5 Battleground States," *Fox News*, September 21, 2010, accessed July 4, 2013 from http://www.foxnews.com/politics/2010/09/21/fox-new s-polls-track-tea-party-influence-battleground-states/.

54 Hendrik Hertzberg, "Electoral Dissonance."

55 Hendrik Hertzberg, "Electoral Dissonance."

56 Jeff Zeleny, "Democrats Sketch Ad Plan for Defending House Seats," *New York Times*, July 22, 2010, accessed July 4, 2013 from http://www.nytimes.com/2010/07/23/us/politics/23dems.html.

57 Rhodes Cook, "Two Different Electorates," *Wall Street Journal* (*Capital Journal*), August 12, 2010, accessed July 4, 2013 from http://blogs.wsj.com/capitaljournal/2010/08/12/two-different-electo rates/.

58 Rhodes Cook, "GOP Leads 'Battle of the Primary Ballots,'" *Wall Street Journal* (*Capital Journal*), July 1, 2010, accessed July 4, 2013 from http://blogs.wsj.com/capitaljournal/2010/07/01/gop-leads-bat tle-of-the-primary-ballots/.

59 Kate Zernike and Megan Thee-Brenan, "Poll Finds Tea Party Backers Wealthier and More Educated."

60 Peter Wallsten and Danny Yadron, "Tea-Party Movement Gathers Strength," *Wall Street Journal*, September 29, 2010, accessed July 4,

2013 from http://online.wsj.com/article/SB1000142405274870388
2404575520252928390046.html.
61 "34% Say They Or Someone Close To Them Part of Tea Party
Movement," *Rasmussen Reports*, April 13, 2010, accessed July 4,
2013 from http://www.rasmussenreports.com/public_content/politi
cs/general_politics/april_2010/34_say_they_or_someone_close_to_
them_part_of_tea_party_movement.
62 Jeff Zeleny, "To Help Democrats in the Fall, Obama May Stay
Away," *New York Times*, July 31, 2010, accessed July 4, 2013 from
http://www.nytimes.com/2010/08/01/us/politics/01obama.html.
63 Tom Leonard, "'I need to do a better job': Humbled Obama offers
olive branch to Republicans after disastrous mid-term defeat," *Mail
Online*, November 4, 2010, accessed July 4, 2013 from http://www.
dailymail.co.uk/news/article-1326243/MID-TERM-ELECTIONS-
2010-Obama-defeat-I-need-better-job.html.
64 CNN Political Unit, "CNN Poll: Obama's job approval rating on the
rise," *CNN Politics (political ticker. . .)*, January 18, 2011, accessed
July 4, 2013 from http://politicalticker.blogs.cnn.com/2011/01/18/
cnn-poll-obamas-job-approval-rating-on-the-rise/.
65 "Poll Chart: Obama Job Approval," *Huffpost Pollster*, n.d., accessed
July 4, 2013 from http://elections.huffingtonpost.com/pollster/
obama-job-approval.

Chapter 3   Re-Inflation

1 Mark Leibovich, "Message Maven Finds Fingers Pointing at Him,"
New York Times, March 6, 2010, accessed July 4, 2013 from http://
www.nytimes.com/2010/03/07/us/politics/07axelrod.html.
2 "Press Conference by the President," *The White House President
Barack Obama*, February 9, 2009, accessed July 4, 2013 from http://
www.whitehouse.gov/the-press-office/press-conference-president.
3 "Remarks by the President at Memorial Service in Honor of Walter
Cronkite," *The White House President Barack Obama*, September
9, 2009, accessed July 14, 2013 from http://www.whitehouse.gov/
the-press-office/remarks-president-memorial-service-honor-walter-
cronkite.
4 Karen Travers, "Exclusive: President Obama: We Lost Touch with
American People Last Year," *ABC World News with Diane Sawyer*,
January 20, 2010, accessed July 4, 2013 from http://abcnews.
go.com/WN/Politics/president-obama-lost-touch-american-people-
year/story?id=9613462#.UbsSRJzX9EI. In the midst of the midterm
election season, during a private meeting with his re-election team,
Obama acknowledged having been out of the game during his

first term – up until that point: "For the last 20 months I have not been political, not played politics. I've got three months before the election. What do I have to do? What's the best use of my time?" (Jonathan Alter, *The Center Holds: Obama and His Enemies*, Simon and Schuster, Kindle Edition, 2013, page 27).

5 Lindsey Boerma, "Obama reflects on his biggest mistake as president," *CBS News*, July 12, 2012, accessed July 4, 2013 from http://www.cbsnews.com/8301-503544_162-57471351-503544/obama-reflects-on-his-biggest-mistake-as-president/.

6 Lindsey Boerma, "Obama reflects on his biggest mistake as president."

7 See, for example, Laura Meckler, "Obama Says He Needs to Tell 'Story' Better," *Wall Street Journal* (*Washington Wire*), July 12, 2012, accessed July 4, 2013 from http://blogs.wsj.com/washwire/2012/07/12/obama-says-he-needs-tell-the-story-better/; Michael Warren, "Obama: My Biggest Mistake Was Not 'Telling a Story' (Updated)," *The Weekly Standard* (*The Blog*), July 12, 2012, accessed July 4, 2013 from http://www.weeklystandard.com/blogs/obama-my-biggest-mistake-was-not-telling-story_648482.html; Mark Trumbull, "Obama says messaging, not policy, was his biggest mistake. Is that true?," *The Christian Science Monitor*, July 13, 2012, accessed July 4, 2013 from http://www.csmonitor.com/USA/Elections/President/2012/0713/Obama-says-messaging-not-policy-was-his-biggest-mistake.-Is-that-true; and Kristen A. Lee, "Obama says first-term failure was not telling a story," *Daily News*, July 13, 2012, accessed July 4, 2013 from http://www.nydailynews.com/news/election-2012/obama-first-term-failure-telling-story-article-1.1113839.

8 "Remarks of First Lady Michelle Obama in Support of Senator Russ Feingold," *The White House President Barack Obama*, October 13, 2010, accessed July 4, 2013 from http://www.whitehouse.gov/the-press-office/2010/10/13/remarks-first-lady-michelle-obama-support-senator-russ-feingold.

9 Kevin Sack, "Black Turnout Will Be Crucial for Democrats."

10 Kevin Sack, "Black Turnout Will be Crucial for Democrats."

11 Matt Bai, "After Detour, a Map of America's Journey," *New York Times*, January 26, 2011, accessed July 4, 2013 from http://www.nytimes.com/2011/01/26/us/politics/26bai.html.

12 Matt Bai, "After Detour, a Map of America's Journey."

13 "The State of the Union 2011: Winning The Future," *The White House President Barack Obama*, n.d., accessed July 4, 2013 from http://www.whitehouse.gov/state-of-the-union-2011.

14 Joe Klein, "Obama's SOTU Success: Making Democrats the

Party of Optimism," *TIME Magazine*, January 27, 2011, accessed July 4, 2013 from http://www.time.com/time/magazine/article/0,9171,2044735,00.html.

15 Although there may have been some hesitation in using the term "political assassination," as *New York Times* op-ed columnist Paul Krugman put it, "the odds are that it was." He pointed out that Giffords had been on Sarah Palin's notorious "crosshairs" list of Democrats to unseat in the 2010 election. (Paul Krugman, "Assassination Attempt in Arizona, *New York Times*, January 8, 2011, accessed June 23, 2013 from http://krugman.blogs.nytimes.com/2011/01/08/assassination-attempt-in-arizona/).

16 Washington Post Staff, "Obama's Tucson speech transcript: Full text," *Washington Post*, January 13, 2011, accessed July 4, 2013 from http://www.washingtonpost.com/wp-dyn/content/article/2011/01/13/AR2011011301532.html.

17 "Arizona Rampage Dominates Public's News Interest: Bipartisan Praise for Obama Memorial Speech," *Pew Research Center for the People & the Press*, January 18, 2011, accessed July 4, 2013 from http://www.people-press.org/2011/01/18/arizona-rampage-dominates-publics-news-interest/.

18 James Dao and Dalia Sussman, "For Obama, Big Rise in Poll Numbers After Bin Laden Raid," *New York Times*, May 4, 2011, accessed July 4, 2013 from http://www.nytimes.com/2011/05/05/us/politics/05poll.html.

19 Sam Schechner, "Obama Drew Big TV Crowd," *Wall Street Journal*, May 4, 2011, accessed July 4, 2013 from http://online.wsj.com/article/SB10001424052748703834804576301821550865988.html.

20 "President Obama's speech on Osama bin Laden's death: President Obama speaks to the nation on Osama bin Laden's killing by U.S. forces in a compound in Pakistan," *Los Angeles Times*, May 2, 2011, accessed July 4, 2013 from http://articles.latimes.com/2011/may/02/nation/la-na-bin-laden-obama-text-20110502.

21 John Harwood, "President, Rebounding, Gives Opponents Pause," *New York Times (The Caucus)*, January 24, 2011, accessed July 4, 2013 from http://thecaucus.blogs.nytimes.com/2011/01/24/president-rebounding-gives-opponents-pause/.

22 John Harwood, "President, Rebounding, Gives Opponents Pause."

23 Congressman Paul Ryan (R-Wisconsin, 1st district), Chair of the House Budget Committee, would become the eventual Republican vice-presidential pick.

24 "Remarks by the President at a Facebook Town Hall," *The White House President Barack Obama*, April 20, 2011, accessed July 4,

2013 from http://www.whitehouse.gov/the-press-office/2011/04/20/remarks-president-facebook-town-hall.

25 "Remarks by the President on Fiscal Policy," *The White House President Barack Obama*, April 13, 2011, accessed July 4, 2013 from http://www.whitehouse.gov/the-press-office/2011/04/13/remarks-president-fiscal-policy.

26 "Remarks by the President on Fiscal Policy."

27 "Remarks by the President on Fiscal Policy."

28 Damian Paletta and Naftali Bendavid, "Parties Trade Jabs Ahead of Talks on Deficit Despite Tough Rhetoric, Signs of Behind-the-Scenes Activity," *Wall Street Journal*, April 15, 2011, accessed July 4, 2013 from http://online.wsj.com/article/SB10001424052748703983104576262932534033722.html.

29 Ryan Grim, "John Boehner Rejects Obama's Grand Bargain On Debt Ceiling," *HuffPost Politics*, July 9, 2011, accessed July 4, 2013 from http://www.huffingtonpost.com/2011/07/09/john-boehner-debt-ceiling_n_893952.html.

30 Greg Sargent, "Obama made the moral case for what it means to be a Democrat," *Washington Post Opinions*, April 13, 2011, accessed July 4, 2013 from http://www.washingtonpost.com/blogs/plum-line/post/obama-made-the-moral-case-for-what-it-means-to-be-a-democrat/2011/03/03/AFq7NrXD_blog.html.

31 Helene Cooper, "Obama's Task: Soothing His Own Stalwarts," *New York Times* (*The Caucus*), April 20, 2011, accessed July 4, 2013 from http://thecaucus.blogs.nytimes.com/2011/04/20/obamas-task-soothing-his-own-stalwarts/.

32 "The Presidential Divider: Obama's toxic speech and even worse plan for deficits and debt," *Wall Street Journal*, April 14, 2011, accessed July 4, 2013 from http://online.wsj.com/article/SB10001424052748703730104576260911986870054.html?mod=WSJ_Opinion_LEADTop.

33 "Paul Ryan Thrashes Obama's Speech: 'Exploiting People's Emotions' Is 'Demagoguery'!" *YouTube*, posted by Greg Hendler on April 13, 2011, accessed July 4, 2013 from http://www.youtube.com/watch?v=WT30c5qbk90.

34 Mark Landler and Helene Cooper, "President Heads West to Sell His Deficit Plan," *New York Times*, April 17, 2011, accessed July 4, 2013 from http://www.nytimes.com/2011/04/18/us/politics/18obama.html.

35 Mark Landler and Helene Cooper, "President Heads West to Sell His Deficit Plan."

36 Jennifer Steinhauer and Carl Hulse, "House G.O.P. Members Face Voter Anger Over Budget," *New York Times*, April 26, 2011,

accessed July 4, 2013 from http://www.nytimes.com/2011/04/27/us/
politics/27congress.html.

37 Richard W. Stevenson, "The Budget Debate, Revealed," *New York
Times*, April 16, 2011, accessed July 4, 2013 from http://www.
nytimes.com/2011/04/17/weekinreview/17deficit.html.

38 See, for example, John Cassidy, "Budget Battles: Advantage Obama,
New Yorker, April 13, 2011, accessed July 4, 2013 from http://
www.newyorker.com/online/blogs/johncassidy/2011/04/budget-
battles-advantage-obama.html; Carol E. Lee and Damian Paletta,
"Obama Stokes Deficit Fight: President Rips GOP Fiscal Plan, Says
Mix of Taxes, Cuts Needed; Foes Dismayed," *Wall Street Journal*,
April 14, 2011, accessed July 4, 2013 from http://online.wsj.com/
article/SB10001424052748703385404576259903446373140.
html; Lori Montgomery, "Obama address was surprise attack,
GOP lawmakers say," *Washington Post*, April 14, 2011, accessed
July 14, 2013 from http://articles.washingtonpost.com/2011-04-
14/business/35230397_1_chicago-fundraisers-president-obama-
obama-allies; Peter Catapano, "An Uncivil War," *New York Times*
(*Opinionator*), April 15, 2011, accessed July 4, 2013 from http://
opinionator.blogs.nytimes.com/2011/04/15/an-uncivil-war/;   and
Robert Creamer, "How Obama Seized the Political High Ground in
Budget War," *HuffPost Politics*, April 14, 2011, accessed July 4, 2013
from   http://www.huffingtonpost.com/robert-creamer/how-obama-
seized-the-poli_b_849122.html.

39 Daniel Henninger, "Who Do You Trust? Obama and Ryan agree:
This is a 'defining moment.'" *Wall Street Journal*, April 14, 2011,
accessed July 4, 2013 from http://online.wsj.com/article/SB1000142
4052748703730104576261241061275206.html.

40 "Documents: The Full Results From The New York Times and
CBS News Poll," *New York Times*, August 4, 2011, accessed July
4, 2013 from http://www.nytimes.com/interactive/2011/08/05/us/
politics/20110805_Poll-docs.html.

41 "Documents: The Full Results From The New York Times and CBS
News Poll." While we indicate here that public support for the Tea
Party had fallen dramatically, and adumbrate the political significance of this decline for the presidential race, this did not mean that
Tea Party influence inside the Republican Party, and especially inside
the Republican Congressional Caucus, was diminished in a com-
mensurate way. Indeed, there emerged an often destructive tension
between the broad public perception of the Tea Party and intra-party
perceptions. This would play out, to the party and Romney's great
detriment, in the attenuated Republican primary contests and the
eventual choice of Ryan as the vice-presidential pick. Arguably, the

"Battle for the Soul of the GOP," as *The Blaze*'s Meredith Jessup declared in a post-election analysis, continues apace ("Meredith Jessup, "Tea Party vs. Progressive Republicans – Battle for the Soul of the GOP," *The Blaze*, December 3, 2012, accessed July 7, 2013 from http://www.theblaze.com/stories/2012/12/03/tea-party-vs-pro gressive-republicans-battle-for-the-soul-of-the-gop/).

42 "More Now Disagree with Tea Party – Even in Tea Party Districts," *Pew Research Center for the People & the Press*, November 29, 2011, accessed August 4, 2013 from http://www.people-press. org/2011/11/29/more-now-disagree-with-tea-party-even-in-tea-party-districts/.

43 There was considerable speculation on the waning support for the Tea Party movement. Some tried suggesting that the decline actually reflected the movement's growing power, noting that established centrist Republicans, like Senator Olympia Snowe of Maine, had begun to court the conservative side (Robert Schlesinger, "The Decline and Fade of the Tea Party," *US News & World Report*, November 30, 2011, accessed August 4, 2013 from http://www.usnews.com/ opinion/articles/2011/11/30/the-decline-and-fade-of-the-tea-party-). Our alternative emphasis – on the broad decline of support for the Tea Party vis-à-vis Obama – was shared even by some staunch Tea Party Activists themselves, who began to distance themselves from the movement at around this time. Andrew Ian Dodge, Snowe's "dark horse" primary challenger and founder of the Maine Tea Party Patriots, told the *Washington Monthly*: "Now I'm emphasizing my Tea Party links even less because a lot of people think they are crazy people who almost drove us off a [fiscal] cliff" (Colin Woodard, "A Geography Lesson for the Tea Party," *Washington Monthly Magazine*, November/December 2011, accessed August 4, 2013 from http://www.washingtonmonthly.com/magazine/novemberdece mber_2011/features/a_geography_lesson_for_the_tea032846. php?page=all).

Others noted the disappointment with how Tea Party-backed representatives actually performed in Washington after being elected. Pointing out that 35 of 60 Tea Party Caucus members voted for the debt-ceiling deal in August, freshman Republican Mick Mulvaney explained: "If you ran as a Tea Party candidate, but got up here and drank the water and didn't vote consistently with the Tea Party principles, I think that might undermine the credibility of the brand. People will be less likely to have continued faith in the Tea Party if they thought it had achieved nothing, or very little" (Emily Miller, "MILLER: Tea Party decline? Limited-government movement remains a political powerhouse," *Washington Times*, December 2,

2011, accessed August 4, 2013 from http://www.washingtontimes. com/news/2011/dec/2/tea-party-decline/#ixzz2azB5xisw). Of course, such extensive Republican support for the debt-ceiling was compelled by Obama's successful symbolic repositioning.

44 "President Obama Speaks About His Debt Reduction Plan," CNN, September 19, 2011, accessed July 4, 2013 from http://transcripts. cnn.com/TRANSCRIPTS/1109/19/se.01.html.

45 Lydia Saad, "New Low of 26% Approve of Obama on the Economy: Ratings on Afghanistan and foreign affairs have also declined," *Gallup Politics*, August 17, 2011, accessed July 4, 2013 from http://www.gallup.com/poll/149042/New-Low-Approve-Obama-Economy.aspx.

46 Lydia Saad, "In U.S., Slight Majority Now Blame Obama for U.S. Economy: Independents lean toward Republicans' view that Obama bears significant blame," *Gallup Politics*, September 21, 2011, accessed July 4, 2013 from http://www.gallup.com/poll/149600/ Slight-Majority-Blame-Obama-Economy.aspx.

47 Jonathan Weisman and Danny Yadron, "President's Ratings Climb," *Wall Street Journal*, January 20, 2011, accessed July 4, 2013 from http://online.wsj.com/article/SB10001424052748704590704576092273958557698.html.

48 "Labor Force Statistics from the Current Population Survey, 2003–2013."

49 "Employment, Hours, and Earnings from the Current Employment Statistics survey (National) 2003–2013, *Bureau of Labor Statistics*, n.d., accessed July 4, 2013 from http://data.bls.gov/timeseries/ CES0000000001.

50 Neil King, Jr. and Scott Greenberg, "Poll Shows Budget-Cuts Dilemma: Many Deem Big Cuts to Entitlements 'Unacceptable,' but Retirement and Means Testing Draw Support," *Wall Street Journal*, March 3, 2011, accessed July 4, 2013 from http://online.wsj.com/ article/SB10001424052748704728004576176741120691736.htm l#project%3DWSJPDF%26s%3Ddocid%253D110302233016-962e97512a5b45d7b64c022c35d65248%257Cfile%253Dwsj-nbc-poll03022011.

51 Jonathan Weisman, "Voter Discontent Deepens Ahead of Obama Jobs Plan," *Wall Street Journal*, September 6, 2011, accessed July 4, 2013 from http://online.wsj.com/article/SB10001424053111903895904576547014053423394.html.

52 Although we have referenced most of the major national polls in one way or another, for the actual "horserace" we have relied heavily on the Electoral College forecasts by Silver, whose initial claim to political fame emerged in the wake of the 2008 election, when, in his

FiveThirtyEight blog, he had predicted correctly not only the overall result but also 49 of the 50 states. In August 2010, Silver's blog became licensed to the *New York Times*. His meteoric rise to political fame continued, with a *New York Times* bestseller, status as one of *TIME Magazine*'s 100 Most Influential People of 2009, and five Webby Awards as the "Best Political Blog" from the International Academy of Digital Arts and Sciences. In the 2012 presidential election, Silver bested his own record and correctly predicted all 50 states. However, Silver wasn't the only poll aggregator in 2012 to show the Electoral College in Obama's favor despite many national polls still depicting the race as too close to call. In fact, on Election Day, all the major poll aggregators – *FiveThirtyEight*, the *Talking Points Memo Poll Tracker*, the *Huffington Post*'s *Pollster*, the *RealClearPolitics Average*, and the *Princeton Election Consortium* – predicted an Electoral College win for Obama, albeit with some variation. But Silver, along with Sam Wang of the Princeton Election Consortium, was the closest with regard to the popular vote, predicting about a 2.5 percentage point margin as compared to the final result of nearly 4 points (Daniel Terdiman, "Can Nate Silver and friends nail their presidential predictions?," *CNET*, November 6, 2012, accessed July 4, 2013 from http://news.cnet.com/8301-13510_3-57545543-21/can-nate-silver-and-friends-nail-their-presidential-predictions/). Although much less known, Wang, a professor of neuroscience at Princeton, was one of the first to engage in the meta-analysis of presidential election polls – in 2004. Like Silver, he had run a blog that concentrated heavily on polling. His prediction for 2008 had actually outstripped Silver's, calling the Electoral College exactly except for one split vote in Nevada. We have incorporated Wang's data for 2012 when they were available; he was not nearly as prolific as Silver, who posted daily, if not more frequently, and began posting much earlier than Wang. We have decided to use numbers from both because their methods were slightly different, each offering pluses and minuses; for further elaboration on their respective models, see chapter 5, note 28.

53 Nate Silver, "The North Dakota Paradox," *New York Times* (*FiveThirtyEight*), September 2, 2011, accessed July 4, 2013 from http://fivethirtyeight.blogs.nytimes.com/2011/09/02/the-north-dakota-paradox/.

54 "CNN/Opinion Research Corporation Poll – Dec 17–19, 2010," n.d., accessed July 4, 2013 from http://i2.cdn.turner.com/cnn/2010/images/12/28/rel17k.pdf.

55 Jennifer Steinhauer, "Hating Incumbency and Incumbents Too," *New York Times*, November 1, 2011, accessed July 4, 2013 from http://

www.nytimes.com/2011/11/02/us/politics/voter-rage-has-congress-worried-about-job-security-its-own.html.
56 "Poll Chart: Obama Job Approval." Even 43 percent was considerably higher than Jimmy Carter, who had an approval rating of 31 percent at a parallel time in his presidency, according to a *Times* and CBS News poll, which also showed Ronald Reagan at 46 percent and the elder George Bush at 70 percent (Jeff Zeleny and Megan Thee-Brenan, "Support for Obama Slips; Unease on 2012 Candidates," *New York Times*, September 16, 2011, accessed July 4, 2013 from http://www.nytimes.com/2011/09/17/us/politics/obamas-support-is-slipping-poll-finds-but-his-jobs-plan-is-well-received.html).
57 According to *New York Times*'s Nate Silver, an average of CNN and *TIME Magazine* polls that asked, "How well are things going in the country today?" revealed that 60 percent felt they were going "very badly" or "pretty badly" (Nate Silver, "The 10-Word Question That Could Cost Obama the Election," *New York Times* (*FiveThirtyEight*), June 6, 2011, accessed July 4, 2013 from http://fivethirtyeight.blogs.nytimes.com/2011/06/06/the-ten-word-question-that-could-cost-obama-the-election/).
58 "How Americans Feel About Congress After the Debt Deal," *New York Times*, August 4, 2011, http://www.nytimes.com/interactive/2011/08/04/us/politics/how-americans-feel-about-congress-after-the-debt-ceiling-deal.html?ref=politics. The technical outcome of this transformation in political fortunes for the Republican Congress was the sequestration agreement passed as part of the Budget Control Act of 2011 and signed by the president on August 2, 2011. Whereas the right had threatened to make the budget a major issue in the 2012 campaign, their willingness to sign on to sequestration implicitly acknowledged their symbolic weakness: They decided to postpone the budget confrontation until after the election, when they would not have to defend their cuts in social spending to the American people in a national election. As it turned out, after the election, the two sides could not reach agreement about budget issues, and sequestration went into effect, on March 1, 2013, with $1.2 trillion of cuts scheduled to kick in to both social spending and the military budget. Polls showed that a majority of the American people continued to support the newly re-elected Democratic president on the issue, opposing sequestration and social budget cuts. An NBC/*Wall Street Journal* poll found that 52 percent thought the sequester cuts were a bad idea, as opposed to 21 percent who thought they were a good idea, and more blamed the Republicans (Mark Murray, "Poll: Public Wary about Sequester Cuts; but Obama in stronger political position than GOP," *First Read on NBCNEWS.com*, February

26, 2013, accessed June 27, 2013 from http://firstread.nbcnews. com/_news/2013/02/26/17105540-nbcwsj-poll-public-wary-about-sequester-cuts-but-obama-in-stronger-political-position-than-gop?lite). Nevertheless, the ultra-conservative block of "Tea Party" Republicans in the House refused to compromise. The ideological fervor of their artfully delimited local constituencies meant that such recalcitrance would not cost these congressional representatives their own re-election. However, Republicans more concerned about national image were not nearly so sanguine, worrying that the Party would suffer the same kind of damage to its future presidential hopes as it had during the 2012 election. Such concerns crystallized during the October, 2013 budget and debt-ceiling face off, when the House Tea Party Caucus held their moderate Republican colleagues and the Democrats hostage, shutting down the government and pushing the US to the edge of fiscal default. Building on the symbolic power over budgetary matters he had amassed during 2011 and ran on during the 2012 campaign, President Obama refused to give in to what he characterized as extremist threats to the wider solidarity of American society. After moderate House Republicans broke from the Tea Party group and supported a bi-partisan debt-ceiling and budget bill, the Republican Party began a debilitating, highly public splintering process, whereas the president emerged from the crisis with his cultural authority intact.

59 Allison Kopicki, "Approval of Congress Matches Record Low," *New York Times* (*The Caucus*), September 16, 2011, accessed July 14, 2013 from http://thecaucus.blogs.nytimes.com/2011/09/16/ approval-of-congress-matches-record-low/.

60 Jonathan Weisman, "Voter Discontent Deepens Ahead of Obama Jobs Plan," *Wall Street Journal*, September 6, 2011, accessed July 4, 2013 from http://online.wsj.com/article/SB1000142405311190389 5904576547014053423394.html.

Chapter 4   Setting the Stage

1 Billy Hallowell, "Obama to Supporters: 'We Were Able to Prevent America From Going Into a Great Depression,'" *The Blaze*, November 8, 2011, accessed July 4, 2011 from http://www.theblaze. com/stories/2011/11/08/obama-to-supporters-we-were-able-to-prevent-america-from-going-into-a-great-depression/.

2 Although Romney remained near the top in many primaries and polls, there was considerable distrust and dislike for him among the conservative core of the Republican Party and especially the Tea Partyers. He was often portrayed as a RINO (Republican in

Name Only) within a party that had "traded in country-club aristocracy for pitchfork populism," as *TIME Magazine*'s Joe Klein put it (Joe Klein, "Outsiders vs. Insiders: The Struggle for the GOP's Soul," *TIME Magazine*, June 16, 2011, accessed July 4, 2013 from http://www.time.com/time/nation/article/0,8599,2077962,00. html#ixzz2XDcotRuu). As the Tea Party Nation website proclaimed during the run-up to the primary season, there was a definite desire for an alternative Republican presidential candidate: "The philosophy of the Tea Party in the primary season can be described in three words. Anybody but Romney" (Judson Phillips, "Anybody but Romney," *Tea Party Nation*, November 1, 2011, accessed July 4, 2013 from http://www.teapartynation.com/forum/topics/anybody-but-romney). *Politico* headlined "Conservative elites pine for 2012 hero" and described the "dull ache" from being "profoundly dissatisfied with the current field" (Jonathan Martin and Ben Smith, "Conservative elites pine for 2012 hero," *Politico*, August 23, 2011, accessed July 4, 2013 from http://www.politico.com/news/stories/0811/61882.html). Ultra-conservative blogger Michelle Malkin referred to the field of candidates as "non-Romneys" (Michelle Malkin, "The abysmal incompetence of the non-Romneys; Huntsman, Gingrich, Perry all go Occupier; Santorum declines," *Michelle Malkin*, January 9, 2012, accessed July 4, 2013 from http://michellemalkin.com/2012/01/09/ the-abysmal-incompetence-of-the-non-romneys/). Summing up the primary contest, *The Nation* ran through the numbers:

> Romney was almost always the front-runner. But he was never loved, or even liked all that much, by Republican voters. Even to the last – in the Wisconsin and Maryland primaries of April 3 – Romney could not get 50 percent of the vote. Republican voters in thirteen primary and caucus states gave wins to someone other than Romney. Four states put Romney in third place. Where Romney did win, it was more often than not by narrow margins – as in battleground states such as Michigan, Ohio and Wisconsin. And though the former governor of Massachusetts built and maintained a steady delegate lead, most Republicans voted for someone else – as of April 3, only 41 percent of GOP primary and caucus voters had backed Romney. The combined vote for other Republicans was roughly 6.6 million to around 4.5 million for Mr. Mitt. (John Nichols, "It's Romney, the GOP Candidate Opposed by 59 Percent of Republicans," *The Nation*, April 10, 2012, accessed July 4, 2013 from http://www.thenation.com/blog/167313/its-romney-gop-candidate-opposed-59-percent-republicans#ixzz2XED7ij1D).

This difficulty in connecting, or fusing, with the Republican core audience and the Tea Party played out during the whole of the primary contest, as partisans turned from one alternative to another – from Herman Cain, Michele Bachmann, and Rick Perry early on to Rick Santorum, Newt Gingrich, and Ron Paul – in the thick of the season. Romney's difficulty in fusing with the core conservative audience also affected his eventual choice of a running mate. Paul Ryan was exactly the sort of hardcore Republican conservative Romney thought he needed to help fire up his base.

3 Jeff Zeleny and Jim Rutenberg, "Romney's Team Prepares for Obama, Too," *New York Times*, November 14, 2011, accessed July 5, 2013 from http://www.nytimes.com/2011/11/15/us/politics/before-primaries-romneys-team-looks-ahead-to-obama.html.

4 "Mitt Romney's America," *YouTube*, posted by prioritiesUSAaction on November 1, 2011, accessed July 5, 2013 from http://www.youtube.com/watch?v=Oz1aLR05eb8.

5 "MittvMitt.com: The story of two men trapped in one body," *YouTube*, posted by DemocraticVideo on November 27, 2011, accessed July 5, 2013 from http://www.youtube.com/watch?v=K9njHHyRI7g.

6 Jonathan Weisman, "Obama, Romney Camps Look Past the Primaries," *Wall Street Journal*, November 27, 2011, accessed July 5, 2013 from http://online.wsj.com/article/SB10001424052970204753404577066723477904922.html.

7 Helene Cooper and Mark Landler, "After Iowa, Obama Campaign Sharpens 2 Negative Portrayals of Romney," *New York Times*, January 4, 2012, accessed July 5, 2013 from http://www.nytimes.com/2012/01/05/us/politics/democrats-target-romney-after-iowa-win.html.

8 Robert Draper, "Building a Better Mitt Romney-Bot," *New York Times Magazine*, November 30, 2011, accessed July 5, 2013 from http://www.nytimes.com/2011/12/04/magazine/mitt-romney-bot.html.

9 Kasie Hunt and Charles Babington, "Mitt Romney: 'I Like Being Able To Fire People' Who Don't Provide Adequate Services," *HuffPost Politics*, January 9, 2012, accessed July 5, 2013 from http://www.huffingtonpost.com/2012/01/09/mitt-romney-i-like-being-able-to-fire-people_n_1194115.html.

10 Benjy Sarlin, "Romney: 'Corporations Are People, My Friend' [VIDEO]," *Talking Points Memo*, August 11, 2011, accessed July 5, 2013 from http://tpmdc.talkingpointsmemo.com/2011/08/romney-corporations-are-people-my-friend-video.php.

11 Mackenzie Weinger, "Mitt Romney: 'I'm not concerned about the very poor,'" *Politico*, February 1, 2012, accessed July 5, 2013 from http://www.politico.com/news/stories/0212/72297.html.

12 Garrett Haake, "In the Granite State, a Romney blitz," *First Read on*

NBCNEWS.com, December 21, 2011, accessed July 5, 2013 from http://firstread.nbcnews.com/_news/2011/12/21/9619598-in-the-granite-state-a-romney-blitz.

13 Matthew Mosk, Brian Ross, and Megan Chuchmach, "Romney Parks Millions in Cayman Islands," *ABC News* (*Nightline*), January 18, 2012, accessed July 5, 2013 from http://abcnews.go.com/Blotter/romney-parks-millions-offshore-tax-haven/story?id=15378566.

14 Neil King, Jr. and Sara Murray, "Romney Battles Likability Deficit," *Wall Street Journal*, January 26, 2012, accessed July 5, 2013 from http://online.wsj.com/article/SB10001424052970204624204577183393793238890.html.

15 "Poll Chart: Barack Obama Favorable Rating," *HuffPost Pollster*, n.d., accessed July 5, 2013 from http://elections.huffingtonpost.com/pollster/obama-favorable-rating; "Poll Chart: Mitt Romney Favorable Rating," *HuffPost Pollster*, n.d., accessed July 5, 2013 from http://elections.huffingtonpost.com/pollster/mitt-romney-favorability.

16 Jonah Goldberg, "Goldberg: Perry's sweet spot: Republican voters want to beat Obama. But they also want to like their candidate. That's a bigger challenge for Mitt Romney than for Rick Perry," *Los Angeles Times*, September 13, 2011, accessed July 5, 2013 from http://articles.latimes.com/2011/sep/13/opinion/la-oe-goldberg-perry-romney-20110913.

17 Thom Riehle, "Romney's Likeability Gap with Obama," *YouGov*, January 22, 2012, accessed July 5, 2013 from http://today.yougov.com/news/2012/01/22/romneys-likeability-gap-obama/.

18 John Sides and Lynn Vavreck, "Does Mitt Romney Have a Wealth Problem?" *YouGov*, January 13, 2012, accessed July 5, 2013 from http://today.yougov.com/news/2012/01/13/does-mitt-romney-have-wealth-problem/.

19 John Sides and Lynn Vavreck, "Does Mitt Romney Have a Wealth Problem?"

20 A. G. Sulzberger, "Obama Strikes Populist Chord With Speech on G.O.P. Turf," *New York Times*, December 6, 2011, accessed July 5, 2013 from "http://www.nytimes.com/2011/12/07/us/politics/obama-strikes-populist-chord-with-speech-in-heartland.html.

21 Peter Wallsten, "Obama plans to turn anti-Wall Street anger on Mitt Romney, Republicans," *Washington Post*, October 14, 2011, accessed July 5, 2013 from http://articles.washingtonpost.com/2011-10-14/politics/35279754_1_new-attack-line-obama-aides-david-plouffe.

22 Jonathan Weisman, "WSJ/NBC Poll: Most Americans Say U.S. Economy Favors 'Small Portion of the Rich,'" *Wall Street Journal*

(*Washington Wire*), November 7, 2011, accessed July 5, 2013 from http://blogs.wsj.com/washwire/2011/11/07/wsjnbc-poll-most-ameri cans-say-u-s-economy-favors-small-portion-of-the-rich/.

23 "Giving Everyone a Fair Shot," *Organizing for Action*, n.d., accessed July 5, 2013 from http://www.barackobama.com/fair-shot?source=homepage-cta.

24 Richard W. Stevenson, "On Tricky Terrain of Class, Contrasting Paths," *New York Times*, July 7, 2012, accessed July 5, 2013 from http://www.nytimes.com/2012/07/08/us/politics/obama-and-rom ney-gamble-on-wealth-divide.html.

25 As conservative blogger Michelle Malkin pointed out, Romney's opponents in the primaries were not immune to capitalizing on the movement: "With his incessant bashing of how the private equity industry works in the real world, Newt [Gingrich] (along with Rick Perry) is morphing into an Occupy Wall Street zealot" ("The abysmal incompetence of the non-Romneys; Huntsman, Gingrich, Perry all go Occupier; Santorum declines Share.")

26 "One sr asked romney abt #occupywallstreet – he responded that he had spoken to ppl involved & 'I think its dangerous – this class warfare,'" *Twitter*, posted by Sarah Boxer on October 4, 2011, accessed July 4, 2013 from https://twitter.com/Sarah_Boxer/status/121299267276128256.

27 Ashley Parker, "Romney Fields Friendly Questions in New Hampshire," *New York Times* (*The Caucus*), October 28, 2011, accessed July 5, 2013 from http://thecaucus.blogs.nytimes.com/2011/10/28/romney-fields-friendly-questions-in-new-hamp shire/.

28 Thomas Lane, "Limbaugh Lashes Romney For Occupy Rhetoric," *Talking Points Memo*, February 23, 2012, accessed July 5, 2013 from http://2012.talkingpointsmemo.com/2012/02/limbaugh-laun ches-into-romney-for-occupy-rhetoric.php.

29 Jeff Zeleny and Jim Rutenberg, "Romney's Team Prepares for Obama, Too."

30 "Giving Everyone a Fair Shot."

31 Michael Barbaro and Nicholas Confessore, "Democrats Descend on Iowa to Hit Romney," *New York Times* (*The Caucus*), January 1, 2012, accessed July 5, 2013 from http://thecaucus.blogs.nytimes.com/2012/01/01/democrats-descend-on-iowa-to-hit-romney/.

32 Douglas Belkin, "Democratic Party Takes on Romney," *Wall Street Journal*, January 2, 2012, accessed July 5, 2013 from http://online.wsj.com/article/SB10001424052970203462304577135862924896 688.html.

33 Douglas Belkin, "Democratic Party Takes on Romney."

34 "Labor Force Statistics from the Current Population Survey, 2003–2013."
35 Josh Mitchell, "Jobless Rates Decline in Key States," *Wall Street Journal*, March 13, 2012, accessed July 5, 2013 from http://online.wsj.com/article/SB10001424052702303717304577279863334347238.html.
36 "Poll Chart: Obama Job Approval."
37 Gerald F. Seib, "Ground Is Shifting Beneath 2012 Race," *Wall Street Journal*, February 14, 2012, accessed July 5, 2013 from http://online.wsj.com/article/SB10001424052970204062704577220991267017900.html.
38 Why the economy was recovering is not our concern here, but, rather, how this economic shift was interpreted. Whether the shift was facilitated by Obama's early stimulus or occurred in spite of it was furiously debated, not only by politicians with ideological interests, but by academic economists. Austerity vs. stimulus is an intra-disciplinary dispute that falls along the Keynes vs. Friedman divide. Its instantiation in the Obama era was triggered when Harvard economists Carmen Reinhart and Kenneth Rogoff circulated their paper, "Growth in a Time of Debt," in 2010. The paper, published in *American Economic Review*, identified a tipping point of 90 percent of government debt to GDP, after which economic growth was supposed to decline. The article quickly achieved canonical status among conservatives opposing Obama's economic policies, and more broadly as well. Even as late as January 27, 2013, for example, a *Washington Post* editorial warned against any relaxation on the deficit front, arguing we are "dangerously near the 90 percent mark that economists regard as a threat to sustainable economic growth" (Editorial Board, "Debt reduction hawks and doves," *Washington Post*, January 27, 2013, accessed June 23, 2013 from http://www.washingtonpost.com/opinions/debt-reduction-hawks-and-doves/2013/01/26/3089bd52-665a-11e2-93e1-475791032daf_story.html).
     Liberal academic economists, who had sharply disputed Reinhart-Rogoff from the beginning, hailed signs of economic recovery as evidence of the paper's scientific falsification. In a *Times* op-ed piece, Nobel laureate Paul Krugman disputed the *Post*'s editorial: "Notice the phrasing: 'economists,' not 'some economists,' let alone 'some economists, vigorously disputed by other economists with equally good credentials', which was the reality." He continues:

As soon as the paper was released, many economists pointed out that a negative correlation between debt and economic performance need not mean that high debt causes low growth. It could just as easily be the other way around, with poor economic performance leading to high debt. Indeed, that's obviously the case for Japan, which went deep into debt only after its growth collapsed in the early 1990s. Over time, another problem emerged: Other researchers, using seemingly comparable data on debt and growth, couldn't replicate the Reinhart-Rogoff results. They typically found some correlation between high debt and slow growth – but nothing that looked like a tipping point at 90 percent or, indeed, any particular level of debt. Finally, Ms. Reinhart and Mr. Rogoff allowed researchers at the University of Massachusetts to look at their original spreadsheet – and the mystery of the irreproducible results was solved. First, they omitted some data; second, they used unusual and highly questionable statistical procedures; and finally, yes, they made an Excel coding error. Correct these oddities and errors, and you get what other researchers have found: some correlation between high debt and slow growth, with no indication of which is causing which, but no sign at all of that 90 percent "threshold." (Paul Krugman, "The Excel Depression," *New York Times*, April 18, 2013, accessed June 23, 2013 from http://www.nytimes.com/2013/04/19/opinion/krugman-the-excel-depression.html)

Despite its practitioners' best efforts, the discipline of economics has not yet achieved the status of a mature science and there is legitimate doubt as to whether it ever will. Whatever an economic observation's claim to reality, it is always just that – a claim. In the performance of politics, reality is in dispute, and not in a scientific way.

An economically focused, materialist interpretation of the election, one held by many political scientists and sociologists, as well as by pundits, would claim, of course, that Obama's rise in approval rating was the first of many indications that Obama's increasing fortunes depended entirely on the falling unemployment rate. Our account does not deny that the economy played a role and, as we note later (see page 81), it certainly is likely that the fall in the final months to 7.8 percent helped Obama's chances for re-election. What we do maintain, however, is that the unemployment rate, by itself, cannot be taken as a predictor of Obama's standing, either in itself or in relation to Romney. In the year before the unemployment rate began to fall, Obama had greatly increased his symbolic power vis-à-vis the Tea Party, Congress, and Romney himself – even as his job approval rating (as compared to the personal likeability rating and many other indicators) held steady or even slightly decreased. While we acknowledge that there may well be a correlation between economic rates and presidential job approval rating, it is not at all clear that this is a causal relationship. It is mediated, at any rate, by notions of heroism and competence, and these latter are affected by the kinds of factors we identify throughout this book. If Obama had performed poorly in cultural terms – losing the 2011 budget wars, failing to frame Romney as a Bain capitalist, blowing the effort to take out Osama bin Laden, failing to recover in the second and third debates – the falling unemployment rate would not have caused his approval rate to rise, and he would in all probability have lost anyway. To maintain that economic developments are causally predictive of electoral outcomes is to write off the entire effort of campaigning as tilting at windmills.

39 Reid J. Epstein and Jim Vandehei, "Mitt Romney and the Bain bomb," *Politico*, January 19, 2012, accessed July 5, 2013 from http://www.politico.com/news/stories/0112/71231.html.

40 Neil King, Jr., "Pro-Gingrich Group Lambasts Romney for 'Predatory' Capitalism," *Wall Street Journal* (*Washington Wire*), January 8, 2012, accessed July 5, 2013 from http://blogs.wsj.com/washwire/2012/01/08/pro-gingrich-group-lambasts-romney-for-predatory-capitalism/.

41 Peter Hamby, "Perry donor defects to Romney, citing Bain attacks," *CNN Politics* (*political ticker...*), January 12, 2012, accessed July 5, 2013 from http://politicalticker.blogs.cnn.com/2012/01/12/perry-donor-defects-to-romney-citing-bain-attacks/.

42 "Decision 2012: candidates fight for Florida: On the trail today Mitt Romney challenged President Barack Obama and Newt Gingrich complained the rules at the NBC News debate limited his performance. NBC's Peter Alexander reports," *NBC Nightly News*, January 24, 2012, accessed July 5, 2013 from http://www.nbcnews.com/video/nightly-news/46122843#46122843.

43 "Mitt Romney Victory Speech," *C-SPAN Video Library*, January 10, 2012, accessed July 5, 2013 from http://www.c-spanvideo.org/clip/4294122.

44 "American Optimism," *YouTube*, posted by mittromney on December 29, 2011, accessed July 5, 2013 from http://www.youtube.com/watch?v=p1TZ_NOI4Bg.

45 Poll Chart: 2012 General Election: Romney vs. Obama, *HuffPost Pollster*, n.d., accessed July 5, 2013 from http://elections.huffingtonpost.com/pollster/2012-general-election-romney-vs-obama.

46 The *New York Times*'s Nate Silver's prediction for the chances of Obama winning against Romney went from 40 percent in November to 60 percent by mid-February (Nate Silver, "The Fundamentals Now Favor Obama," *New York Times* (*FiveThirtyEight*), February 15, 2012, accessed July 5, 2013 from http://fivethirtyeight.blogs.nytimes.com/2012/02/15/the-fundamentals-now-favor-obama/).

47 Michael D. Shear, "For Romney's Trusted Adviser, 'Etch A Sketch' Comment Is a Rare Misstep," *New York Times*, March 21, 2012, accessed July 5, 2013 from http://www.nytimes.com/2012/03/22/us/politics/etch-a-sketch-remark-a-rare-misstep-for-romney-adviser.html.

48 Gregory Wallace, "Etch A Sketch comment no child's play," *CNN Politics (political ticker...)*, March 21, 2012, accessed July 5, 2013 from http://politicalticker.blogs.cnn.com/2012/03/21/video-romney-adviser-on-fall-campaign-everything-changes-its-almost-like-an-etch-a-sketch/.

49 Michael D. Shear, "For Romney's Trusted Adviser, 'Etch A Sketch' Comment Is a Rare Misstep."

50 Michael D. Shear, "For Romney's Trusted Adviser, 'Etch A Sketch' Comment Is a Rare Misstep."

51 Nate Silver, "Etch A Sketch Highlights Missed Opportunities for Romney's Rivals," *New York Times (FiveThirtyEight)*, March 23, 2012, accessed July 5, 2013 from http://fivethirtyeight.blogs.nytimes.com/2012/03/23/etch-a-sketch-highlights-missed-opportunities-for-romneys-rivals/.

52 Daniel Horowitz, "Mitt Romney: The Consummate Etch A Sketch," *Red State*, March 21, 2012, accessed July 7, 2013 from http://www.redstate.com/2012/03/21/mitt-romney-the-consummate-etch-a-sketch/.

53 Helene Cooper, "In Strategy Shift, Obama Team Attacks Romney From the Left," *New York Times*, April 20, 2012, accessed July 5, 2013 from http://www.nytimes.com/2012/04/21/us/politics/campaign-memo-in-strategy-shift-obama-team-attacks-romney-from-the-left.html.

Chapter 5   Unfolding the Drama

1 Richard W. Stevenson, "Political Memo: His Attack Plan Set, Obama Seeks Positives," *New York Times (The Caucus)*, April 14, 2012, accessed July 4, 2013 from http://query.nytimes.com/gst/fullpage.html?res=9C04E5DD1131F937A25757C0A9649D8B63.

2 Mark Landler and Michael D. Shear, "Obama Formally Kicks Off Campaign in Ohio and Virginia," *New York Times*, May 6, 2012, accessed June 23, 2013 from http://www.nytimes.com/2012/05/06/us/politics/obama-holds-large-campaign-rallies-in-ohio-and-virginia.html. This phrase would become a campaign mantra.

3 "The Road We've Traveled," *YouTube*, posted by Barack Obamadotcom on March 15, 2012, accessed July 5, 2013 from http://www.youtube.com/watch?v=2POembdArVo.

4 "President Obama at the first 2012 rally: 'We're moving this country forward,'" *YouTube*, posted by BarackObamadotcom on May 8, 2012, accessed July 5, 2013 from https://www.youtube.com/watch?v=1pOmavZ_3DU.

5 Michael Cohen, "Mitt Romney, retro-conservative: In 2008, Obama won the presidency on the promise of 'change'. Romney hopes to win 2012 promising the reverse. Can it work?" *The Guardian*, April 30, 2012, accessed July 5, 2013 from http://www.guardian.co.uk/commentisfree/cifamerica/2012/apr/30/mitt-romney-retro-conserva tive.

6 Michael D. Shear, "Republicans Assail Obama in Wake of Disappointing Jobs Report," *New York Times (The Caucus)*, June 1, 2012, accessed July 5, 2013 from http://thecaucus.blogs.nytimes. com/2012/06/01/republicans-assail-obama-in-wake-of-disappoint ing-jobs-report/.

7 Michael D. Shear, "Republicans Assail Obama in Wake of Disappointing Jobs Report."

8 "We've Heard it All Before – Obama for America Television Ad," *YouTube*, posted by BarackObamadotcom on June 4, 2012, accessed July 5, 2013 from http://www.youtube.com/watch?v=o WdZEJW1vWY.

9 "Mitt Romney Criticizes President Obama For Wanting To Hire More Police, Firemen and Teachers," *You Tube*, posted by cub-merdu on June 8, 2012, accessed July 5, 2013 from http://www. youtube.com/watch?v=LoSmWK_-x4g. The ostensible "message" of Wisconsin was that Americans might support spending cuts even if they hurt workers, and increased unemployment, in the public sector. Republican governor Scott Walker, who had proposed such cuts (along with the suspension of collective bargaining rights), was the first governor in US history to survive a recall election, winning by a definitive margin of 53 percent vs. 46 percent (Monica Davey and Jeff Zeleny, "Walker Survives Wisconsin Recall Vote," *New York Times*, June 5, 2012, accessed July 5, 2013 from http://www.nytimes. com/2012/06/06/us/politics/walker-survives-wisconsin-recall-effort. html).

10 Michael D. Shear, "Democrats Hit Romney on 'Message of Wisconsin' Comments," *New York Times (The Caucus)*, June 8, 2012, accessed July 5, 2013 from http://thecaucus.blogs.nytimes.com/2012/06/08/ democrats-hit-romney-on-message-of-wisconsin-comments/. In the American colloquial, "first responders" had been applied to police and firefighters, especially in the wake of 9/11, when they had courageously rushed to the burning Twin Towers and had suffered devastation as a result.

11 "One Chance," *YouTube*, posted by BarackObamadotcom on April 27, 2012, accessed July 5, 2013 from http://www.youtube.com/watch?v=BD75KOoNR9k.

12 Ben Feller, "Obama Campaign Using Osama Bin Laden Killing As 2012 Campaign Tool," *HuffPost Politics*, April 28, 2012, accessed July 5, 2013 from http://www.huffingtonpost.com/2012/04/28/obama-campaign-bin-laden_n_1461431.html.

13 Toby Harnden, "SEALs slam Obama for using them as 'ammunition' in bid to take credit for bin Laden killing during election campaign," *Mail Online*, April 30, 2012, accessed July 5, 2013 from http://www.dailymail.co.uk/news/article-2137636/Osama-bin-Laden-death-SEALs-slam-Obama-using-ammunition-bid-credit.html.

14 Toby Harnden, "SEALs slam Obama for using them as 'ammunition.'"

15 "Statement by the President on the Supreme Court's Ruling on Arizona v. the United States," *The White House President Barack Obama*, June 25, 2012, accessed July 5, 2013 from http://www.whitehouse.gov/the-press-office/2012/06/25/statement-president-supreme-court-s-ruling-arizona-v-united-states.

16 Lucy Madison, "Romney on immigration: I'm for 'self-deportation,'" *CBS News*, January 24, 2012, accessed July 5, 2013 from http://www.cbsnews.com/8301-503544_162-57364444-503544/romney-on-immigration-im-for-self-deportation/.

17 David Jackson, "Obama, critics praise different parts of immigration ruling," *USA Today* (*The Oval*), June 25, 2012, accessed July 5, 2013 from http://content.usatoday.com/communities/theoval/post/2012/06/justices-divided-on-arizona-immigration-law/1#.UbwsLZzX9EI.

18 Helene Cooper and Ashley Parker, "Obama Calls Romney Possible 'Outsourcer in Chief,'" *New York Times*, June 26, 2012, accessed July 5, 2013 from http://www.nytimes.com/2012/06/27/us/politics/obama-calls-romney-potential-outsourcer-in-chief.html.

19 "Obama for America TV Ad: 'Revealed – VA,'" *YouTube*, posed by BarackObamadotcom on June 26, 2012, accessed July 5, 2013 from http://www.youtube.com/watch?v=P78E_iMu9Qo.

20 David Jackson, "Obama jabs Romney over outsourcing vs. off-shoring," *USA Today* (*The Oval*), June 25, 2012, accessed July 5, 2013 from http://content.usatoday.com/communities/theoval/post/2012/06/obama-jabs-romney-over-outsourcing-offshoring/1#.Ubws1ZzX9EI.

21 Mary Bruce, "President Obama Slams Mitt Romney's Record on Outsourcing," *ABC News*, June 22, 2012, accessed July 5, 2013

from http://abcnews.go.com/blogs/politics/2012/06/president-obam
a-slams-mitt-romneys-record-on-outsourcing/.

22 "No Evidence," *YouTube*, posted by mittromney on July 12,
2012, accessed July 5, 2013 from http://www.youtube.com/watch?
v=L6b9F9IiAZw.

23 Michael D. Shear, "Romney Seeks Obama Apology for Bain Attacks,"
New York Times, July 13, 2012, accessed July 5, 2013 from http://
www.nytimes.com/2012/07/14/us/politics/romney-demands-apol-
ogy-from-obama-on-bain-allegations.html.

24 See for example, Rex Nutting, "'No, It's You. You're the Outsourcer,'"
Wall Street Journal, July 14, 2012, accessed July 5, 2013 from http://
online.wsj.com/article/SB10001424052702304373804577521280
104610596.html; Patrick O'Connor and Peter Nichols, "The Murky
Calculus of Job Exports: Obama Camp Warns Romney Would Be
'Outsourcer-in-Chief,' Draws Accusations of Sophistry," *Wall Street
Journal*, June 29, 2012, accessed July 5, 2013 from http://online.
wsj.com/article/SB10001424052702304830704577496622302951
632.html; Michael D. Shear and Richard A. Oppel, Jr., "Obama and
Romney Trade Shots, a Few Possibly Accurate, on Outsourcing,"
New York Times, July 10, 2012, accessed July 5, 2013 from http://
www.nytimes.com/2012/07/11/us/politics/obama-and-romney-
trade-shots-a-few-possibly-accurate-on-outsourcing.html; and Trip
Gabriel, "Accusing Obama of Untruths Over Outsourcing," *New
York Times*, July 12, 2012, accessed July 5, 2013 from http://www.
nytimes.com/2012/07/13/us/politics/accusing-obama-of-untruths-
over-outsourcing.html.

25 "Obama's 'Outsourcer' Overreach: The president's campaign fails to
back up its claims that Romney 'shipped jobs' overseas," *FactCheck.
org*, June 29, 2012, accessed July 5, 2013 from http://factcheck.
org/2012/06/obamas-outsourcer-overreach/.

26 Rex Nutting, "'No, It's You. You're the Outsourcer.'" For a time,
the Romney campaign sought to portray president Obama as the
"outsourcer-in-chief," with the Republican National Committee
implying on a website entitled "obamanomicsoutsourced.com" that
some of the 2009 stimulus money actually went to companies oper-
ating overseas. According to the *New York Times*, "several of the
companies cited on the new site said the Republican characteriza-
tions of their activities were far from accurate" (Michael D. Shear
and Richard A. Oppel, Jr., "Obama and Romney Trade Shots").

27 Colleen McCain Nelson, "Political Perceptions: Campaigns Dance
Around 'Liar,'" *Wall Street Journal* (*Washington Wire*), July 13, 2012,
accessed July 5, 2013 from http://blogs.wsj.com/washwire/2012/07/13/
political-perceptions-campaigns-dance-around-liar/.

28 This complex, seemingly paradoxical situation was reflected in the
   New York Times's poll analyst Nate Silver's more nuanced understanding of both national and state level polling data. Silver showed
   Obama had a 68.3 percent chance of winning at this juncture (Nate
   Silver, "July 3: No Polling Fireworks on Eve of Holiday," *New York
   Times* [*FiveThirtyEight*], July 3, 2012, accessed July 5, 2013 from
   http://fivethirtyeight.blogs.nytimes.com/2012/07/03/july-3-no-poll
   ing-fireworks-on-eve-of-holiday/).
       Silver could discern Obama's position more accurately because of
   the sophistication of his predictive model. First, while sites such as *Real
   Clear Politics* took a straight average of polls, Silver's *FiveThirtyEight*
   drew a weighted average of polls based on their past accuracy as well
   as their methodological standards. Second, Silver offered a detailed
   forecast regarding each candidate's chances of winning the Electoral
   College on Election Day, much like InTrade and other "prediction"
   markets. As he described it, "The forecast works by running simulations ... designed to consider the uncertainty in the outcome at the
   national level and in individual states. It recognizes that voters in each
   state could be affected by universal factors – like a rising or falling
   economic tide – as well as by circumstances particular to each state.
   Furthermore, it considers the relationships between the states and the
   ways they might move in tandem with one another." And although
   the model relied "fairly heavily" on polling, it also considered an
   index of national economic conditions that takes into account job
   growth, personal income, industrial production, consumption, infla-
   tion, the change in the S&P 500 stock market index, and the consensus forecast of gross domestic product growth over the next two
   economic quarters. It also considered "house effects" or partisan bias,
   which tended to run toward Republicans among national pollsters
   like Gallup or Rasmussen and toward Democrats among state-level
   pollsters, and adjusted for differences in polls taken of "likely voters"
   vs. "registered voters." Finally, Silver also offered a "now-cast," which
   utilized the same information but reflected what would happen if the
   election were held "today" (Nate Silver, "Election Forecast: Obama
   Begins With Tenuous Advantage," *New York Times* [*FiveThirtyEight*],
   June 7, 2012, accessed July 5, 2013 from http://fivethirtyeight.blogs.
   nytimes.com/2012/06/07/election-forecast-obama-begins-with-tenu
   ous-advantage/).
       Like Silver, Sam Wang of the *Princeton Election Consortium*
   offered "now-cast" style predictions, beginning in July, along with
   a popular vote "Meta-Margin" defined as "how much swing would
   have to take place to generate a near-exact electoral tie," defining "the Popular Meta-Margin is equivalent to the two-candidate

difference found in most single polls" (Sam Wang, "About the Meta-Analysis (FAQ)," *Princeton Election Consortium*, September 19, 2012, accessed July 5, 2013 from http://election.princeton.edu/faq/#metamargin). The primary difference from Silver's modeling is that Wang did not add in economic indicators, offering two reasons: "First, to my knowledge it is not definitively demonstrated that those variables add new information beyond what is already present in polls. Second, it is ineluctably true that they will add uncertainty" (Sam Wang, "Presidential prediction (Take 2)," *Princeton Election Consortium*, August 8, 2012, accessed July 5, 2013 from http://election.princeton.edu/2012/08/08/presidential-prediction-take-2/). Second, Wang used only state polls, because they have shown to be relatively unbiased. Finally, Wang also aggregated the polls without weighting them, asserting that "selecting polls leads to unintended biases" (Sam Wang, "Electoral College Meta-Analysis (election. princeton.edu)," n.d., accessed July 5, 2013 from http://synapse. princeton.edu/~sam/pollcalc.html#sources). Because of the lack of uncertainty, Wang showed Obama as doing considerably better throughout the four months of his coverage of the race – not just better than many national polls but better than Silver's now-cast. As early as July 8, Wang gave Obama 8 to 1 odds of winning ("Obama 318 EV popular +3.0% Meta +3.7%; House Dem win 91%; Senate toss-up!" *Princeton Election Consortium*, July 8, 2012, accessed July 5, 2013 from http://election.princeton.edu/2012/07/08/election-2012-coverage-is-under-construction/#more-3485).

Yet, even as both Silver and Wang showed Obama consistently ahead as compared with other polls, their forecasts ebbed and flowed according to major events in both campaigns, as they were constructed and interpreted by campaigns and audiences. As we will see, even for these forecasters, there were moments when their number-crunching put the Republican campaign ahead, revealing the outcome of the election to be far from determined.

29 These numerical measures of connection and solidarity would mirror the eventual exit polling. When voters were asked "Who is more in touch with people like you?" 53 percent replied Obama, as compared to 43 percent for Romney ("President: Full Results," *CNN*, December 10, 2012, accessed July 5, 2013 from http://edition. cnn.com/election/2012/results/race/president#exit-polls).

30 Jeffrey M. Jones, "Obama Has Big Likability Edge Over Romney: Nearly twice as many say Obama, rather than Romney, is more likable," *Gallup*, May 8, 2012, accessed July 5, 2013 from http:// www.gallup.com/poll/154547/obama-big-likability-edge-romney. aspx.

31 Jeffrey M. Jones, "Likability Top Characteristic for Both Romney and Obama: Eighty-one percent say Obama is likable; 64% say Romney is," *Gallup*, June 26, 2012, accessed July 5, 2013 from http://www.gallup.com/poll/155351/Likability-Top-Characteristic-Romney-Obama.aspx.

32 John Sides, "Romney's 'Empathy Gap,'" *New York Times* (*FiveThirtyEight*), April 11, 2012, accessed July 5, 2013 from http://fivethirtyeight.blogs.nytimes.com/2012/04/11/romneys-empathy-gap/.

33 This strategy reflected a shift from focusing on personal attacks against Obama. Almost a year of focus groups with undecided and "sometimes torn" voters held by Romney's super PAC Crossroads had revealed that "the harshest anti-Obama jabs backfire with most Americans." Larry McCarthy, the producer behind the infamous Willie Horton commercial in 1988 whom the *New York Times* referred to as one of the "most fearsome players in Republican politics," explained: "Criticizing President Obama is a challenging proposition in terms of ads because a lot of your swing voters this year voted for him in 2008. They genuinely liked him, they thought he had the right message, they thought he was different" (Jeremy W. Peters, "Subtler Entry From Masters of Attack Ads," *New York Times*, May 22, 2012, accessed July 5, 2013 from http://www.nytimes.com/2012/05/22/us/politics/new-crossroads-gps-ad-takes-a-soft-shot-at-obama.html).

34 "Priorities USA Action: 'Briefcase,'" *YouTube*, posted by priorities USAaction on June 28, 2012, accessed July 5, 2013 from http://www.youtube.com/watch?v=6uMlsQ9HiFo.

35 "Obama for America TV Ad: 'Makes You Wonder,'" *YouTube*, posted by BarackObamadotcom on July 17, 2012, accessed July 5, 2013 from http://www.youtube.com/watch?v=uMo5pykT4uw.

36 efowler, "Presidential Ads 70 Percent Negative in 2012, Up from 9 Percent in 2008," *Wesleyan Media Project*, May 2, 2012, accessed July 5, 2013 from http://mediaproject.wesleyan.edu/2012/05/02/jump-in-negativity/.

37 Donovan Slack, "RIP positive ads in 2012," *Politico*, November 14, 2012, accessed July 5, 2013 from http://www.politico.com/news/stories/1112/83262.html.

38 "'Doing Fine' – Restore Our Future," *YouTube*, posted by RestoreOurFuture on June 20, 2012, accessed July 5, 2013 from http://www.youtube.com/watch?v=FNES9N0mmEU.

39 "Obama for America TV Ad: 'Firms,'" *YouTube*, posted by BarackObamadotcom on July 14, 2012, accessed July 5, 2013 from http://www.youtube.com/watch?v=Ud3mMj0AZZk.

40 Peggy Noonan, "About Those 2012 Political Predictions: The Romney campaign in September seemed like a 'rolling calamity.' In retrospect this holds up nicely," *Wall Street Journal*, December 28, 2012, accessed July 5, 2013 from http://online.wsj.com/article/SB10 001424127887324669104578205714173777172.html.

41 "Remarks by the President on Supreme Court Ruling on the Affordable Care Act," *The White House President Barack Obama*, June 28, 2012, accessed July 5, 2013 from http://www.whitehouse.gov/the-press-office/2012/06/28/remarks-president-supreme-court-ruling-affordable-care-act.

42 "Mitt Romney reacts to the health care ruling," *YouTube*, posted by CNN on June 28, 2012, accessed July 5, 2013 from http://www.youtube.com/watch?v=dCJH6p3UcFs.

43 Allison Kopicki, "Nation's Verdict: Americans Split on Health Ruling," *New York Times (The Caucus)*, July 4, 2012, accessed July 5, 2013 from http://query.nytimes.com/gst/fullpage.html?res=9D00E 1DA153DF937A35754C0A9649D8B63.

44 Richard W. Stevenson, "On Tricky Terrain of Class, Contrasting Paths," *New York Times*, July 7, 2012, accessed July 5, 2013 from http://www.nytimes.com/2012/07/08/us/politics/obama-and-romney-gamble-on-wealth-divide.html.

45 "Remarks by the President at a Campaign Event in Roanoke, Virginia," *The White House President Barack Obama*, July 13, 2012, accessed July 5, 2013 from http://www.whitehouse.gov/the-press-office/2012/07/13/remarks-president-campaign-event-roanoke-vir ginia.

46 "Remarks by the President at a Campaign Event in Roanoke, Virginia."

47 Trip Gabriel and Peter Baker, "Romney and Obama Resume Economic Attacks, Despite a Few Diversions," *New York Times*, July 17, 2012, accessed July 5, 2013 from http://www.nytimes.com/2012/07/18/us/politics/romney-and-obama-resume-economic-attacks.html.

48 "These Hands," *YouTube*, posted by mittromney on July 19, 2012, accessed July 5, 2013 from http://www.youtube.com/watch?v=4Lr49t4-2b8.

49 "'Always' – Obama for America TV Ad," *YouTube*, posted by BarackObamadotcom on July 24, 2012, accessed July 5, 2013 from https://www.youtube.com/watch?v=Z0yK5NakN2o.

50 Kimberly A. Strassel, "Four Little Words: Why the Obama campaign is suddenly so worried," *Wall Street Journal*, July 26, 2012, accessed July 5, 2013 from http://online.wsj.com/article/SB10000872396390 4439314045775513440018773450.html.

51 "Obama for America TV Ad: 'Firms.'"
52 Kimberly A. Strassel, "Four Little Words."
53 Trip Gabriel, "With a Little Theater, Romney Uses Obama's Words Against Him," *New York Times* (*The Caucus*), July 18, 2012, accessed July 5, 2013 from http://thecaucus.blogs.nytimes.com/2012/07/18/ with-a-little-theater-romney-uses-obamas-words-against-him/.
54 Garrett Haake and Michael O'Brien, "Romney surrogate Sununu: 'I wish this president would learn how to be an American,'" *First Read on NBCNEWS.com*, July 17, 2012, accessed July 5, 2013 from http://firstread.nbcnews.com/_news/2012/07/17/12791391-romney-surrogate-sununu-i-wish-this-president-would-learn-how-to-be-an-american?chromedomain=leanforward&lite.
55 "Extended interview: Brian Williams speaks with Mitt Romney: NBC's Brian Williams interviews Republican presidential candidate Mitt Romney on a wide range of topics including the Olympics, gun control, education, taxes and religion," *NBC Nightly News*, July 25, 2012 http://www.nbcnews.com/video/nightly-news/48326 969#48326969.
56 Adam Gabbatt, "Oh, Mitt: those Romney gaffes in full: Boobs, blunders, clangers – whatever you call them, Romney likes to drop them. And he's really outdone himself in London," *The Guardian* (*US News Blog*), July 26, 2012, accessed July 5, 2013 from http:// www.guardian.co.uk/world/us-news-blog/2012/jul/26/mitt-romney-britain-gaffes.
57 Steve Benen, "Putting a value on a people," *MSNBC* (*The Maddow Blog*), July 30, 2012, accessed July 5, 2013 from http://maddowblog. new.msnbc.com/_news/2012/07/30/13034303-putting-a-value-on-a-people,
58 Steve Holland, "Polish Solidarity distances itself from Romney visit," *Reuters*, July 30, 2012, accessed July 5, 2013 from http:// www.reuters.com/article/2012/07/30/us-usa-romney-poland-idIN BRE86T0W820120730?irpc=932.
59 Sebastian Fischer and Christina Hebel, "Tour de Gaffes: Romney Flops in Europe," *Spiegel Online International*, July 31, 2012, accessed July 5, 2013 from http://www.spiegel.de/international/ world/missteps-abound-during-mitt-romney-s-europe-trip-a-847 421.html.
60 Eugene Robinson, "Romney tour '12 – gaffepalooza," *Washington Post*, July 31, 2012, accessed July 5, 2013 from http://www.washing-tonpost.com/opinions/eugene-robinson-romney-stumbles-through-his-world-tour/2012/07/30/gJQAdJJILX_story.html.
61 Jean-Sébastien Stehli, "Mitt Romney est-il un loser?" *Le Figaro* (*Obama Zoom*), July 30, 2012, accessed July 5, 2013 from http://

blog.lefigaro.fr/obamazoom/2012/07/mitt-romney-est-il-un-loser.
html.

62 Graeme Wilson, "Mitt the twit: Wannabe US President Romney in
Games insult, but David Cameron insists: We'll show you," *The Sun*,
July 27, 2012, accessed July 5, 2013 from http://www.thesun.co.uk/
sol/homepage/news/politics/4456840/Wannabe-US-President-Mitt-
Romney-in-Olympics-insult-but-David-Cameron-insists-Well-show-
you.html.

63 Mark Gollom, "How gaffe-filled was Mitt Romney's foreign adven-
ture?" *CBC News*, July 31, 2012, accessed July 5, 2013 from http://
www.cbc.ca/news/world/story/2012/07/31/romney-foreign-trip.
html.

64 Olivier Knox, "Obama Aide: Romney 'Struck Out Playing T-Ball' on
Foreign Trip," *ABC News*, July 31, 2012, accessed July 5, 2013 from
http://abcnews.go.com/Politics/OTUS/obama-aide-romney-struck-
playing-ball-foreign-trip/story?id=16899897#.Ubw36pzX9EI.

65 Scott Wilson and Philip Rucker, "The strategy that paved a winning
path," *Washington Post*, November 7, 2012, accessed July 15, 2013
from http://www.washingtonpost.com/politics/decision2012/the-str
ategy-that-paved-a-winning-path/2012/11/07/0a1201c8-2769-
11e2-b2a0-ae18d6159439_story.html.

66 Nate Silver, "Aug. 9: National Polls Shouldn't Panic Romney," *New
York Times (FiveThirtyEight)*, August 9, 2012, accessed July 5, 2013
from http://fivethirtyeight.blogs.nytimes.com/2012/08/09/aug-9-na
tional-polls-shouldnt-panic-romney/.

67 Sam Wang, "A bad July for Romney," *Princeton Election Consortium*,
August 1, 2012, accessed July 5, 2013 from http://election.princeton.
edu/2012/08/01/a-bad-july-for-romney/#more-3704.

68 "Be Not Afraid," *YouTube*, posted by mittromney on August
9, 2012, accessed July 5, 2013 from http://www.youtube.com/
watch?v=IMv28sYQzCY.

69 "Obama and Romney Discuss Faith in Washington National
Cathedral magazine: Cathedral Age interviewed presidential candidates on 'faith in America,'" *Washington National Cathedral*, August
21, 2012, accessed July 5, 2013 from http://www.nationalcathedral.
org/press/PR-5QLKM-RU000F.shtml. To the surprise of many observers, Romney's identification with the Mormon faith did not become
a campaign issue, even though a substantial minority of Americans
indicated they would not vote for a Mormon candidate – 24 percent
of Democrats and 10 percent of Republicans (Frank Newport, "Bias
Against a Mormon Presidential Candidate Same as in 1967; Four in
10 Americans do not know that Mitt Romney in a Mormon," *Gallup*,
June 21, 2012, accessed June 23, 2013 from http://www.gallup.com/

poll/155273/Bias-Against-Mormon-Presidential-Candidate-1967. aspx). This may have been for the reason noted by John G. Turner, a religious studies professor at George Mason University: "Only the truly paranoid can foresee a Mormon takeover beyond the horizon of a Romney victory." Turner observes that, by contrast, a quarter of the country was Catholic in 1960, when John F. Kennedy's faith was a much larger issue (John G. Turner, "Mitt Romney's Mormon religion a non-issue during the 2012 presidential election," *Washington Post*, October 3, 2012, accessed June 23, 2013 from http://articles. washingtonpost.com/2012-10-03/local/35499803_1_mormonism-lds-church-protestants). But larger issues of civility and confidence about the boundary between politics and religion were also in play. David Axelrod stated explicitly in May of 2012 that the campaign repudiated the idea that Mormonism should be on the table, telling CNN's Candy Crowley that it wasn't "fair game" ("State of the Union with Candy Crowley," *CNN*, May 20, 2012, accessed June 23, 2013 from http://transcripts.cnn.com/TRANSCRIPTS/1205/20/ sotu.01.html).

70 "Tea Time at the Republican National Convention: 'Young gun' VP candidate Paul Ryan rails against President Obama, ignites crowd," *ABC News*, August 29, 2012, accessed July 5, 2013 from http:// abcnews.go.com/Nightline/video/tea-time-republican-national-convention-17112178.

71 Fred Barnes, "How Ryan Recasts the Race: With his big ideas, the GOP's vice presidential candidate makes the incumbent president seem smaller," *Wall Street Journal*, August 20, 2012, accessed July 5, 2013 from http://online.wsj.com/article/SB1000087239639044398 9204577601254048147454.html.

72 Niall Ferguson, "Obama's Gotta Go," *Newsweek Magazine*, August 19, 2012, accessed July 5, 2013 from http://www.thedailybeast.com/ newsweek/2012/08/19/niall-ferguson-on-why-barack-obama-needs-to-go.html. Italics in the original.

73 Fred Barnes, "How Ryan Recasts the Race."

74 Dan Spencer, Romney's magnificent Ryan roll out continues," *Red State*, August 12, 2012, accessed July 7, 2013 from http://www.red state.com/2012/08/12/1115/.

75 Peter Baker, "Ryan Pick Gives Obama Chance to Change Subject," *New York Times*, August 11, 2013, accessed July 5, 2013 from http:// www.nytimes.com/2012/08/12/us/politics/ryan-pick-gives-obama-chance-to-change-subject.html.

76 Nate Silver, "Aug. 14: The Fog of Polling – and Ryan's 'Bounce' So Far," *New York Times* (*FiveThirtyEight*), August 14, 2012, accessed July 5, 2013 from http://fivethirtyeight.blogs.nytimes.

com/2012/08/14/aug-14-the-fog-of-polling-and-ryans-bounce-so-far/. At the one-week mark, the Princeton Election Consortium's Sam Wang also reported a bounce, although he charted its rise to 3–3.6 points by its peak, which occurred just a week later. This divergence represents a rare moment when Wang's numbers were more favorable to Romney than Silver's. Wang was quick to point out, however, that, in spite of any bounce, Obama still retained a 1.8-point lead (Sam Wang, "A better August for Romney," *Princeton Election Consortium*, August 24, 2012, accessed July 5, 2013 from http://election.princeton.edu/2012/08/24/romneys-better-august/).

77 "What do Floridians think about the Romney–Ryan plan to end Medicare as we know it?" *YouTube*, posted by BarackObamadotcom on August 13, 2012, accessed July 5, 2013 from http://www.youtube.com/watch?v=A4OACnOKkbk.

78 "Paid In," *YouTube*, posted by mittromney on August 14, 2012, accessed July 5, 2013 from http://www.youtube.com/watch?v=l4gPvToKTWU.

79 Janet Hook and Damian Paletta, "Selection Sets Off Debate on Government," *Wall Street Journal*, August 13, 2012, accessed July 5, 2013 from http://online.wsj.com/article/SB100008723963904440427045775855800439900456.html.

Chapter 6   Pulling Ahead

1 Nancy Benac and Jennifer Agiesta, AP-GfK Poll: Call them maybes; a fourth of voters undecided or soft supporters of Obama, Romney," AP-GfK, August 25, 2012, accessed July 5, 2013 from http://ap-gfkpoll.com/uncategorized/our-latest-poll-findings-9. The truly "undecided," however, represented a very small percentage of likely voters, about 7 percent. That figure narrowed to just 5 percent in the AP-GfK poll taken just before the election, on October 26 (Connie Cass and Jennifer Agiesta, "AP-GfK Poll: Why can't they decide? Some voters just tuning in, some still mulling, others not that into it, *AP GFK*, October 26, 2012, accessed July 14, 2013 from http://ap-gfkpoll.com/uncategorized/ap-gfk-poll-why-cant-they-decide-some-voters-just-tuning-in-some-still-mulling-others-not-that-into-it). What is more remarkable is just how small this number of voters is if one considered only the battleground states, the too-close-to-call states whose presidential voting would determine the electoral outcome. In an analysis for *Newsweek* magazine, Paul Begala laid out the scenario:

> The truth is, the election has already been decided in perhaps as many as 44 states, with the final result coming down to the half-dozen states that

remain. [N]ot everyone in those closely divided states will make an electoral difference. We can almost guarantee that 48 percent of each state's
voters will go for Obama, and another 48 percent will decide for Romney.
And so the whole shootin' match comes down to around 4 percent of the
voters in six states. I did the math so you won't have to. Four percent of
the presidential vote in Virginia, Florida, Ohio, Iowa, New Mexico, and
Colorado is 916,643 people. That's it. The American president will be
selected by fewer than half the number of people who paid to get into a
Houston Astros home game last year. ("Paul Begala on the Swing Voters
Who Will Pick the President," *Newsweek*, July 16, 2012, accessed July 14,
2013 from http://www.thedailybeast.com/newsweek/2012/07/15/paul-
begala-on-the-swing-voters-who-will-pick-the-president.html)

See chapter 7, note 41, for an additional discussion of the undecided
or truly "independent" voter.
2 David Brooks, "Party of Strivers," *New York Times*, August 30, 2012,
   accessed July 5, 2013 from http://www.nytimes.com/2012/08/31/
   opinion/party-of-strivers.html.
3 Peggy Noonan, "About Those 2012 Political Predictions."
4 "President Barack Obama's Remarks at the 2012 Democratic
   National Convention – Full Speech," *YouTube*, posted by Barack
   Obamadotcom on September 6, 2012, accessed July 5, 2013 from
   http://www.youtube.com/watch?v=2rl8Ou84s5U.
5 "President Barack Obama's Remarks at the 2012 Democratic
   National Convention."
6 Jeff Zeleny, "New Focus for Romney on Connecting and Closing the
   Empathy Gap," *New York Times*, August 10, 2012, accessed July 5,
   2013 from http://www.nytimes.com/2012/08/11/us/politics/romney-
   renews-focus-on-empathy-gap-with-obama.html.
7 Jeff Zeleny, "New Focus for Romney."
8 Jeff Zeleny, "New Focus for Romney."
9 Jim Rutenberg and Jeff Zeleny, "In a Tactical Test, Romney Stakes
   Hopes on Ohio," *New York Times*, September 1, 2012, accessed June
   23, 2013 from http://www.nytimes.com/2012/09/02/us/politics/in-a-
   tactical-test-mitt-romney-stakes-hopes-on-ohio.html.
10 Nate Silver, "Sept. 3: Par or Bogey?" *New York Times*
   (*FiveThirtyEight*), September 4, 2012, accessed July 5, 2013 from
   http://fivethirtyeight.blogs.nytimes.com/2012/09/04/sept-3-par-or-
   bogey/.
11 Sam Wang, "The GOP convention negative bounce: a final look,"
   Princeton Election Consortium, September 7, 2012, accessed July
   5, 2013 from http://election.princeton.edu/2012/09/07/the-gop-con-
   vention-negative-bounce-a-final-look/.

12 Nate Silver, "Sept. 7: Polls Find Hints of Obama Convention Bounce," *New York Times* (*FiveThirtyEight*), September 7, 2012, accessed July 5, 2013 from http://fivethirtyeight.blogs.nytimes.com/2012/09/07/sept-7-polls-find-hints-of-obama-convention-bounce/.

13 Nate Silver, "Oct. 28: In Swing States, a Predictable Election?" *New York Times* (*FiveThirtyEight*), October 29, 2012, accessed July 5, 2013 from http://fivethirtyeight.blogs.nytimes.com/2012/10/29/oct-28-in-swing-states-a-predictable-election/.

14 "Poll Chart: 2012 General Election."

15 Nate Silver, "Sept. 27: The Impact of the '47 Percent,'" *New York Times* (*FiveThirtyEight*), September 28, 2012, accessed July 5, 2013 from http://fivethirtyeight.blogs.nytimes.com/2012/09/28/sept-27-the-impact-of-the-47-percent/. At the same time, conservative polling pundits were performing their own analysis of some of the polls that put Obama ahead in the race. In an op-ed for the *Washington Examiner*, Dean Chambers accused a CNN/ORC poll of being "doubly skewed. It massively under-samples independents while it also over-samples Democratic voters" (Dean Chambers, "Mitt Romney would lead eight in unskewed data from newest CNN/ORC poll," *examiner.com*, September 10, 2012, accessed July 8, 2013 from http://www.examiner.com/article/mitt-romney-would-lead-eight-unskewed-data-from-newest-cnn-orc-poll). Two days later, *The Blaze* followed suit and headlined, "Is The Media Exaggerating Obama's Lead?," also disputing the CNN poll (Mytheos Holt, "Is The Media Exaggerating Obama's Lead?" *The Blaze*, September 12, 2012, accessed July 8, 2013 from http://www.theblaze.com/stories/2012/09/12/is-the-media-exaggerating-obamas-lead/). This marked the beginning of the Republican campaign's public misreading, if not misrepresentation, of polling data (see chapter 7, note 64). Whether it was bad polling or misrepresentation, the misleading results produced public avowals of confidence, which, after the election, many would characterize as evidence that Romney staffers and pollsters were in a state of denial about the shifting currents we are describing here.

16 "Remarks by the President in Golden, CO," *The White House President Barack Obama*, September 13, 2012, accessed July 5, 2013 from http://www.whitehouse.gov/the-press-office/2012/09/13/remarks-president-golden-co.

17 Associated Press, "Romney calls Obama administration's early response to attacks a disgrace," *Fox News*, September 12, 2013 from http://www.foxnews.com/politics/2012/09/11/romney-calls-obama-administration-early-response-to-attacks-disgrace/.

18 Jackie Kucinich, "Romney softens tone on foreign policy," *USA*

Today, September 14, 2012, accessed July 5, 2013 from http://usatoday30.usatoday.com/news/politics/story/2012/09/14/romney-avoids-criticism-of-obama-on-egypt-and-libya/57777740/1.

19 Danny Yadron, "WSJ/NBC Poll: Obama's Approval on Foreign Policy Falls," *Wall Street Journal* (*Washington Wire*), September 18, 2012, accessed July 5, 2013 from http://blogs.wsj.com/washwire/2012/09/18/wsjnbc-poll-obamas-approval-on-foreign-policy-falls/.

20 Nate Silver, "Sept. 27: The Impact of the '47 Percent.'"

21 "Table – Obama for America TV Ad," *YouTube*, posted by BarackObamadotcom on September 26, 2012, accessed July 5, 2013 from http://www.youtube.com/watch?v=ZYI7qPO5wVw.

22 Arielle Hawkins, "Obama outlines plan for the next four years," *CNN Politics* (*political ticker...*), September 27, 2012, accessed July 5, 2013 from http://politicalticker.blogs.cnn.com/2012/09/27/obama-outlines-plan-for-the-next-four-years/.

23 Laura Meckler and Colleen McCain Nelson, "Candidates Exchange Barbs on Patriotism," *Wall Street Journal*, September 27, 2012, accessed July 5, 2013 from http://online.wsj.com/article/SB100008 72396390444549204578022771028647746.html.

24 Nate Silver, "Sept. 27: The Impact of the '47 Percent.'"

25 Peter Kafka, "Mitt Romney Goes Viral," *All Things D*, September 18, 2012, accessed July 5, 2013 from http://allthingsd.com/20120918/mitt-romney-goes-viral/.

26 Indeed, Fred Shapiro, Yale Law School librarian and author, rated the quote number one on his seventh annual "most notable quotations of the year" (Associated Press, "Romney's '47%' chosen as year's best quote," *USA Today*, December 14, 2012, accessed July 5, 2013 from http://www.usatoday.com/story/news/nation/2012/12/09/romneys-47-percent-chosen-as-years-best-quote/1756833/).

27 David Corn, "SECRET VIDEO: Romney Tells Millionaire Donors What He REALLY Thinks of Obama Voters. When he doesn't know a camera's rolling, the GOP candidate shows his disdain for half of America," *MotherJones*, September 17, 2012, accessed July 5, 2013 from http://www.motherjones.com/politics/2012/09/secret-video-romney-private-fundraiser.

28 David Corn, "SECRET VIDEO."

29 "Messina on Romney: 'It's hard to serve as president ... when you've disdainfully written off half the nation.' http://OFA.BO/Qkjfn6," *Twitter*, posted by Barack Obama on September 17, 2012, accessed July 5, 2013 from https://twitter.com/BarackObama/status/247821443537174529. Scott Prouty, a bartender serving at the fundraiser that fateful evening, expressed similar concerns when

he finally went public as the procurer of the video. Describing himself as a "regular guy – middle class, hard-working guy," he pointed to Romney's inability to understand the lives of most Americans: "I don't think he has any clue what a regular American goes through on a daily basis . . . the day in–day out struggles of everyday Americans. That guy has no idea, no idea, and I don't think he'll ever have an idea." Prouty shared how he felt a tugging at his conscience to release the video. "I felt an obligation . . . I felt like it was my duty to make sure as many people heard it as possible" ("The Man Behind the 47% Video," *MSNBC* (*The Ed Show*) March 14, 2013, accessed July 15, 2013 from http://www.nbcnews.com/id/45755822/ns/msnbc-the_ed_show/vp/51170895#51170895).

30 "Who Doesn't Pay Federal Taxes?" *Tax Policy Center Urban Institute and Brookings Institution*, n.d., accessed July 5, 2013 from http://www.taxpolicycenter.org/taxtopics/federal-taxes-households.cfm.

31 William Kristol, "A Note on Romney's Arrogant and Stupid Remarks," *The Weekly Standard* (*The Blog*), September 18, 2012, accessed July 5, 2013 from http://www.weeklystandard.com/blogs/note-romney-s-arrogant-and-stupid-remarks_652548.html.

32 Jim Rutenberg and Ashley Parker, "Romney Says Remarks on Voters Help Clarify Position," *New York Times*, September 18, 2012, accessed July 6, 2013 from http://www.nytimes.com/2012/09/19/us/politics/in-leaked-video-romney-says-middle-east-peace-process-likely-to-remain-unsolved-problem.html.

33 Josh Barro, "Today, Mitt Romney Lost the Election," *Bloomberg News*, September 18, 2012, accessed July 6, 2013 from http://www.bloomberg.com/news/2012-09-17/today-mitt-romney-lost-the-election.html.

34 "Mitt Romney Responds to Leaked Private Fundraiser Video; Comments on Low Income Obama Supporters," *YouTube*, posted by ABC News on September 17, 2012, accessed July 6, 2013 from http://www.youtube.com/watch?v=LWjE5rtYOoo.

35 "Mitt Romney Responds to Leaked Private Fundraiser Video."

36 "Priorities USA Action: 'Doors,'" *YouTube*, posted by prioritiesUSAaction on September 19, 2012, accessed July 6, 2013 from http://www.youtube.com/watch?v=uaKIeR4Sn3k.

37 "Priorities USA Action: 'Doors.'"

38 "My Job – Obama for America TV Ad," *YouTube*, posted by BarackObamadotcom on September 27, 2012, accessed July 6, 2013 from http://www.youtube.com/watch?v=B9xCCaseop4.

39 CBS/AP, "Obama rebukes Romney in Letterman interview," *CBS News*, September 18, 2012, accessed July 6, 2013 from http://www.

cbsnews.com/8301-250_162-57515473/obama-rebukes-romney-in-letterman-interview/.

40 "Obama: Romney hasn't 'gotten around a lot,'" *USA Today* (*The Oval*), September 20, 2012, accessed July 6, 2013 from http://content. usatoday.com/communities/theoval/post/2012/09/20/obama-courts-young-hispanic-voters/70000803/1#.UbxByJzX9EI.

41 Nate Silver, "Sept. 27: The Impact of the '47 Percent.'"

42 Sam Wang, "Vast liberal conspiracies?" *Princeton Election Consortium*, September 26, 2012, accessed July 6, 2013 from http://election.princeton.edu/2012/09/26/vast-liberal-conspirac ies/#more-6246. Nate Silver's Electoral College forecast moved up to 83.9 percent (Nate Silver, "Sept. 27: The Impact of the '47 Percent.'").

43 Jim Rutenberg and Jeff Zeleny, "Polls Show Obama Is Widening His Lead in Ohio and Florida," *New York Times*, September 26, 2012, accessed July 6, 2013 from http://www.nytimes.com/2012/09/26/us/ politics/polls-show-obama-widening-lead-in-ohio-and-florida.html.

44 Jim Rutenberg and Jeff Zeleny, "Polls Show Obama Is Widening His Lead."

45 Jim Rutenberg and Jeff Zeleny, "Polls Show Obama Is Widening His Lead."

46 Jeff Zeleny and Megan Thee-Brenan, "Poll Finds Obama Is Erasing Romney's Edge on Economy," *New York Times*, September 14, 2012, accessed July 6, 2013 from http://www.nytimes.com/2012/09/15/us/ politics/obama-erases-romneys-edge-on-economy-poll-finds.html.

47 Jeff Zeleny and Megan Thee-Brenan, "Poll Finds Obama Is Erasing Romney's Edge."

48 Gerald F. Seib, "A Debate Aimed at the Center, Minus the Fireworks," *Wall Street Journal*, October 5, 2012, accessed July 6, 2013 from http://online.wsj.com/article/SB100008723963904436354045780 35152466253868.html.

Chapter 7   Harrowing Home Stretch

1 For example, the *New York Times* offered a reprise of "memorable" debate moments "that helped define the candidates, for better or worse." They ranged from a "sweaty, shifty, and baggy-eyed" Nixon in 1960 to John McCain's reference to Obama as "that one" in 2008 (Leslye Davis, Jon Huang, and Alexis Mainland, "Will You Smile or Cringe? It Depends," *New York Times*, October 1, 2012, accessed July 6, 2013 from http://www.nytimes.com/interactive/2012/10/02/ us/politics/debate-moments.html?_r=1&).

2 "D.C. Bureau: Romney's Big Break," *Wall Street Journal Live*, October 5, 2012, accessed July 6, 2013 from http://live.wsj.com/video/

dc-bureau-romneys-big-break/6E5EB101-74CB-4E16-AD55-666
04848C4FF.html#!6E5EB101-74CB-4E16-AD55-66604848C4FF.

3 Albert R. Hunt, "In Debates, Obama Must Hide His Scorn," *New York Times*, September 30, 2012, accessed July 6, 2013 from http://www.nytimes.com/2012/10/01/us/01iht-letter01.html.

4 Albert R. Hunt, "In Debates, Obama Must Hide His Scorn."

5 Brian Stelter, "Presidential Debate Drew More Than 70 Million Viewers," *New York Times* (*Media Decoder*), October 4, 2012, accessed July 6, 2013 from http://mediadecoder.blogs.nytimes.com/2012/10/04/presidential-debate-drew-more-than-70-million-viewers/.

6 Peggy Noonan, "Noonan: Romney Deflates the President: The first debate was a surprise. Now the challenger has to prepare for more surprises," *Wall Street Journal*, October 12, 2012, accessed July 6, 2013 from http://online.wsj.com/article/SB1000087239639044422310457803690205933174 8.html.

7 James Taranto, "Honey, I Shrunk the President: Journalists and pundits turn on Obama for failing to make their fairy tales come true," *Wall Street Journal*, October 4, 2012, accessed July 6, 2013 from http://online.wsj.com/article/SB10000872396390443768804578036490415028514.html.

8 Michael D. Shear, "Debate Praise for Romney as Obama Is Faulted as Flat," *New York Times*, October 4, 2012, accessed July 6, 2013 from http://www.nytimes.com/2012/10/05/us/politics/after-debate-a-torrent-of-criticism-for-obama.html?_r=1&.

9 "This is a rolling calamity for Obama. He's boring, abstract, and less human-seeming than Romney!," *Twitter*, posted by Andrew Sullivan on October 3, 2012, accessed July 6, 2013 from https://twitter.com/sullydish/statuses/253671952122785792.

10 "i can't believe i'm saying this, but Obama looks like he DOES need a teleprompter," *Twitter*, posted by Bill Maher on October 3, 2012, accessed July 6, 2013 from https://twitter.com/billmaher/status/253680489850892289.

11 Brian Stelter, "Not Waiting for Pundits' Take, Web Audience Scores the Candidates in an Instant," *New York Times*, October 4, 2012, accessed September 20, 2013 from http://www.nytimes.com/2012/10/04/us/politics/on-twitter-and-apps-audience-at-home-scores-the-debate.html.

12 Peter Nicholas, "Romney Presses Edge After Obama Stumble: President Rallies Support as Rival Looks to Build on Debate," *Wall Street Journal*, October 5, 2012, accessed July 6, 2013 from http://online.wsj.com/article/SB100008723963904437688045780365828573337750.html.

13 CNN Political Unit, "From the spin room . . . ," *CNN Politics* (*political ticker. . .*), October 4, 2012, accessed July 6, 2013 from http://politicalticker.blogs.cnn.com/2012/10/04/from-the-spin-room/comment-page-1/.

14 Mark Landler and Peter Baker, "After Debate, Obama Team Tries to Regain Its Footing," *New York Times*, October 4, 2012, accessed July 6, 2013 from http://www.nytimes.com/2012/10/05/us/politics/obama-team-tries-to-change-course-after-debate-disappoints.html.

15 Mark Landler and Peter Baker, "After Debate, Obama Team Tries to Regain Its Footing."

16 Laura Meckler, "Obama Camp Attacks on Debate 'Dishonesty,'" *Wall Street Journal* (*Washington Wire*), October 5, 2012, accessed July 6, 2013 from http://blogs.wsj.com/washwire/2012/10/05/obama-camp-attacks-on-debate-dishonesty/.

17 "Press Gaggle by Press Secretary Jay Carney and Senior Advisor David Plouffe, 10/4/2012," *The White House President Barack Obama*, October 4, 2012, accessed July 6, 2013 from http://www.whitehouse.gov/the-press-office/2012/10/04/press-gaggle-press-sec retary-jay-carney-and-senior-advisor-david-plouffe.

18 Michael D. Shear, "Debate Praise for Romney."

19 Nate Silver, "Oct. 12: Romney Debate Gains Show Staying Power," *New York Times* (*FiveThirtyEight*), October 12, 2012, accessed July 6, 2013 from http://fivethirtyeight.blogs.nytimes.com/2012/10/12/oct-12-romney-debate-gains-show-staying-power/.

20 Sam Wang, "An apology to poll-dissecters [*sic*]," *Princeton Election Consortium*, October 9, 2012, accessed July 6, 2013 from http://election.princeton.edu/2012/10/09/an-apology-to-poll-sniffers/#more-7210.

21 "Romney's Strong Debate Performance Erases Obama's Lead: GOP Challenger Viewed as Candidate with New Ideas," *Pew Research Center for the People & the Press*, October 8, 2012, accessed July 6, 2013 from http://www.people-press.org/2012/10/08/romneys-strong-debate-performance-erases-obamas-lead/.

22 "Romney's Strong Debate Performance."

23 Jackie Calmes, "Before a Broader Audience, Romney Changes His Tone," *New York Times* (*The Caucus*), October 4, 2012, accessed July 6, 2013 from http://thecaucus.blogs.nytimes.com/2012/10/04/on-the-debate-stage-romney-the-moderate/.

24 "Romney's Strong Debate Performance."

25 Colleen McCain Nelson, "Romney: Debate Showed Obama Is Out of Ideas," *Wall Street Journal* (*Washington Wire*), October 4, 2012, accessed July 6, 2013 from http://blogs.wsj.com/wash wire/2012/10/04/romney-debate-showed-obama-is-out-of-ideas/.

26 Colleen McCain Nelson, "Romney: Debate Showed Obama Is Out of Ideas."
27 Jackie Calmes, "Before a Broader Audience."
28 "VIDEO: Mitt Romney, Paul Ryan Sit Down With Sean Hannity in First Interview Since Debate," *Fox News (Insider)*, October 4, 2012, accessed July 6, 2013 from http://foxnewsinsider.com/2012/10/04/video-mitt-romney-paul-ryan-sit-down-with-sean-hannity-in-first-interview-since-debate.
29 Ashley Parker, "Romney, Buoyed by Debate, Shows Off His Softer Side," *New York Times*, October 6, 2012, accessed July 6, 2013 from http://www.nytimes.com/2012/10/07/us/politics/mitt-romney-after-debate-success-shows-softer-side.html.
30 Mary Bruce, "Obama Will Be More 'Aggressive' in Second Debate, Axelrod Says," *ABC News (Political Punch)*, October 14, 2012, accessed July 6, 2013 from http://abcnews.go.com/blogs/poli tics/2012/10/obama-will-be-more-aggressive-in-second-debate-axel rod-says/.
31 Ian Schwartz, "Obama Defends Performance At Debate: 'I Was Just Too Polite,'" *Real Clear Politics Video*, October 10, 2012, accessed July 6, 2013 from http://www.realclearpolitics.com/video/2012/10/10/obama_defends_performance_at_debate_i_was_just_too_polite.html.
32 "Judging the Candidates' Body Langauge [*sic*]," *Wall Street Journal Live*, October 17, 2013, accessed July 6, 2013 from http://live.wsj.com/video/judging-the-candidates-body-langauge/F8E7148B-70A6-4176-BEB9-3BE262BE9D96.html#!F8E7148B-70A6-4176-BEB9-3BE262BE9D96.
33 "Judging the Candidates' Body Langauge [*sic*]."
34 Alessandra Stanley, "In Debate's Dance, Romney Has More Missteps," *New York Times*, October 17, 2012, accessed July 6, 2013 from http://www.nytimes.com/2012/10/17/us/politics/in-debates-dan ce-romney-has-more-missteps.html. As suggested by these verbal references to visuality and iconic figures, aesthetic forms played a powerful role in communicating cultural meanings throughout the campaign. As one contributor to *Red State* described: "While many of us would prefer that political campaigns were run on issues, the fact is that most are won or lost based on imagery" (streiff [Diary], "Dispatches From the Meme Wars: Part III," *Red State*, May 4, 2012, accessed July 7, 2013 from http://www.redstate.com/2012/05/04/dispatches-from-the-meme-wars-part-iii/).

In a report entitled "Images, Themes, and Props," the *New York Times* analyzed all the campaign ads that ran on television between October 4 and October 21, including those produced by outside groups. They found, for example, that downcast eyes were connected to the economic crisis by Democrats, but to unemployment and taxes by Republicans. Both campaigns used color images of sunny skies to indicate hopes for good times, and black-and-white photos or video when making negative accusations. When they talked about the need for additional job creation, both campaigns displayed visuals of manual workers wearing hard hats and safety goggles. Obama ads most often deployed the American flag in a brightly lit, positive manner, while Romney's ads often cast the flag in gloomy light and portrayed it as damaged in some material way (Amanda Cox, Sergio Peçanha, and Alicia DeSantis, "Images, Themes and Props in Presidential Campaign Ads," *New York Times*, October 25, 2012, accessed July 6, 2013 from http://www.nytimes.com/interac tive/2012/10/25/us/politics/campaign-ads.html).

As this discussion suggests, while such iconic images are omnipresent, the specific meanings of these forms had to be specified in spoken and written discourse. Such discursive meanings are our focus here.

35 "Judging the Candidates' Body Langauge [*sic*]."
36 Andrea Drusch, "Romney and Obama went head to head in the second debate," *Politico Photo Gallery*, October 20, 2012, accessed July 6, 2013 from http://www.politico.com/gallery/2012/10/this-week-in-photos/000492-006756.html.
37 Christopher Santarelli, "'Real News': Debate Was a Fight, But Did Crowley Deliver the TKO?" *The Blaze*, October 17, 2012, accessed July 6, 2013 from http://www.theblaze.com/stories/2012/10/17/real-news-debate-was-a-fight-but-did-crowley-deliver-the-tko/.
38 Peter Baker, "For the President, Punch, Punch, Another Punch," *New York Times*, October 17, 2012, accessed July 6, 2013 from http://www.nytimes.com/2012/10/17/us/politics/in-second-debate-obama-strikes-back.html.
39 Mark Landler and Richard A. Oppel, Jr., "Obama and Romney Keep Up Attacks After Debate," *New York Times*, October 17, 2012, accessed July 6, 2013 from http://www.nytimes.com/2012/10/18/us/politics/obama-team-believes-he-reset-the-race.html.
40 Jon Healy, "Presidential debate Round 2: Fantastic theater but not decisive politics," *Los Angeles Times*, October 16, 2012, accessed July 6, 2013 from http://www.latimes.com/news/opinion/opinion-la/la-ol-presidential-debate-two-winner-20121016,0,3767518.story.
41 To many observers, it hardly seemed possible that at this late date in the campaign, a swath of voters still claimed to be undecided. Jon Stewart crystallized the mystery of such persons – and the subtle sense of antagonism toward them – in a joke on the *Daily Show*,

asking in an exasperated way, "Who are these people and how can they still be undecided?" And Stephen Colbert, on *The Colbert Report*, spoke of the "illusive, mysterious, undecided voters." Sass and Alexander address this apparent conundrum:

> Thomas Jefferson once wrote, "if I could not go to heaven but with a party, I would not go there at all," but, in the contemporary U.S., voting is mostly voting for parties, and parties are viewed at once as the vehicles of democracy and anathema to it. For the Founding Fathers, parties were associated with faction. They represented particularism and division rather than universality, collaboration, and the common good. According to that classically "republican" understanding, the ancient democrat of yore could be committed to democracy and still exhibit independence of thought, whereas the modern democrat, committed to party, was thought lacking the independence required of responsible citizenship. In contemporary American politics, each side of the moral dichotomy between commitment and independence has the capacity to be interpreted both positively and negatively. Commitment can be construed as "capture" or "dependence," but the idea that voters insist on remaining "independent" can signify "irresolution" or even "irresponsibility." This cultural anxiety helps to explain why a growing number of voters have declared themselves to be independent of party commitment, when, in fact, a vastly smaller percentage actually is. When self-declared independents are subjected to the "branching format" question, which asks them which party they lean towards, most independents readily nominate a party. What's more, when the voting records of these independents are examined, it turns out that the party they nominated is also the party for which they reliably vote. Of the 40% of American voters who describe themselves as independent, about 90% readily nominate a party they lean towards, and these 90% usually vote for this party. Thus, the number of "truly independent" voters is vanishingly small – it was recently estimated to be 5% (Larry M. Bartells and Lynn Vavreck, "Meet the Undecided," *New York Times*, July 30, 2012, accessed June 27, 2013 from http://campaignstops. blogs.nytimes.com/2012/07/30/meet-the-undecided/). And a good proportion of these "truly independent" voters are people who do not follow current affairs, making their electoral decisions in the polling booth itself (Philip D. Dalton, *Swing Voters: Understanding Late-Deciders in Late-Modernity*, Cresskill: Hampton Press, 2006). (Jensen Sass and Jeffrey C. Alexander, "American Voters between Commitment and Independence," Unpublished manuscript, 2012)

42 Laura Meckler, Sara Murray, and Carol E. Lee, "Romney, Obama Hone Their Debate Messages," *Wall Street Journal*, October 15,

2012, accessed July 6, 2013 from http://online.wsj.com/article/SB10 000872396390443624204578058991451447924.html.

43 Sarah Dutton, Jennifer De Pinto, Anthony Salvanto, Fred Backus, and Lindsey Boerma, "Poll: Obama edges Romney in second debate," *CBS News Polls*, October 16, 2012, accessed July 6, 2013 from http://www.cbsnews.com/8301-250_162-57533850/poll-obama-edges-romney-in-second-debate/.

44 Sarah Dutton, Jennifer De Pinto, Anthony Salvanto, Fred Backus, and Lindsey Boerma, "Poll: Uncommitted voters say Romney wins debate," *CBS News Polls*, October 3, 2012, accessed July 6, 2013 from http://www.cbsnews.com/8301-250_162-57525698/poll-uncom mitted-voters-say-romney-wins-debate/.

45 Nate Silver, "Oct. 15: Distracted by Polling Noise," *New York Times* (*FiveThirtyEight*), October 15, 2012, accessed July 6, 2013 from http://fivethirtyeight.blogs.nytimes.com/2012/10/15/oct-15-dis tracted-by-polling-noise/.

46 Sam Wang, "Ro-mentum watch: John Dickerson, CBS/Slate," *Princeton Election Consortium*, October 26, 2012, accessed November 7, 2013 from http://election.princeton.edu/2012/10/26/ ro-mentum-watch-john-dickerson-cbsslate/.

47 The strongly pugnacious performance of Joe Biden in the vice-presidential debate, which came in between the first and second presidential debates, may have been a factor as well.

48 "Labor Force Statistics from the Current Population Survey, 2003–2013."

49 Nate Silver, "Oct. 19: After Romney Gains, Should Obama Concede Florida?" *New York Times* (*FiveThirtyEight*), October 20, 2012, accessed July 6, 2013 from http://fivethirtyeight.blogs.nytimes. com/2012/10/20/oct-19-after-romney-gains-should-obama-concede-florida/.

50 Sam Wang, "Presidential discussion thread," *Princeton Election Consortium*, October 22, 2012, accessed July 6, 2013 from http://election.princeton.edu/2012/10/22/presidential-discussion-thread/#more-7809.

51 Ashley Killough, "Obama camp previews foreign policy debate with new ad," *CNN Politics* (*political ticker...*), October 22, 2012, accessed July 6, 2013 from http://politicalticker.blogs.cnn. com/2012/10/22/obama-camp-previews-foreign-policy-debate-with-new-ad/.

52 Janet Hook, "Rivals Seek Points by Going Off-Topic," *Wall Street Journal*, October 23, 2012, accessed July 6, 2013 from http://online. wsj.com/article/SB10001424052970203400604578073641073478 184.html.

53 Carol E. Lee, Janet Hook, and Julian E. Barnes, "Rivals Duel in Final Face-Off: Obama Calls Romney 'Reckless'; Romney Seeks Stronger Global Role for U.S.," *Wall Street Journal*, October 23, 2012, accessed July 6, 2013 from http://online.wsj.com/article/SB10 001424052970203406404578072592934794944.html.
54 Peter Baker and Helene Cooper, "Sparring Over Foreign Policy, Obama Goes on the Offense," *New York Times*, October 22, 2012, accessed July 6, 2013 from http://www.nytimes.com/2012/10/23/us/ politics/obama-and-romney-meet-in-foreign-policy-debate.html.
55 Carol E. Lee, Janet Hook, and Julian E. Barnes, "Rivals Duel in Final Face-Off."
56 Federal News Service, "Transcript of the Third Presidential Debate," *New York Times*, October 22, 2012, accessed July 6, 2013 from http://www.nytimes.com/2012/10/22/us/politics/transcript-of-the-third-presidential-debate-in-boca-raton-fla.html.
57 Federal News Service, "Transcript of the Third Presidential Debate."
58 Federal News Service, "Transcript of the Third Presidential Debate."
59 "Sarah Dutton, Jennifer De Pinto, Anthony Salvanto, Fred Backus, and Lindsey Boerma, "Poll: Decisive win for Obama in final debate," *CBS News Polls*, October 22, 2012, accessed July 6, 2013 from http://www.cbsnews.com/8301-250_162-57537795/poll-decisive-win-for-obama-in-final-debate/.
60 Nate Silver, "Obama Unlikely to Get Big Debate Bounce, but a Small One Could Matter," *New York Times (FiveThirtyEight)*, October 23, 2012, accessed July 6, 2013 from http://fivethirtyeight.blogs. nytimes.com/2012/10/23/obama-unlikely-to-get-big-debate-bounce-but-a-small-one-could-matter/.
61 Nate Silver, "Oct. 12: Romney Debate Gains Show Staying Power," *New York Times (FiveThirtyEight)*, October 12, 2012, accessed July 6, 2013 from http://fivethirtyeight.blogs.nytimes.com/2012/10/12/ oct-12-romney-debate-gains-show-staying-power/.
62 Nate Silver, "Oct. 24: In Polls, Romney's Momentum Seems to Have Stopped," *New York Times (FiveThirtyEight)*, October 25, 2012, accessed July 6, 2013 from http://fivethirtyeight.blogs.nytimes. com/2012/10/25/oct-24-in-polls-romneys-momentum-seems-to-have-stopped/.
63 Sam Wang, "David Brooks – now with Ro-mentum!" *Princeton Election Consortium*, October 25, 2012, accessed July 6, 2013 from http://election.princeton.edu/2012/10/25/do-you-understand-polls-as-well-as-david-brooks/.
64 So, evidently, did the Republican campaign's own insider polls, which may even have placed their candidate in the lead, according to post-election leaks from those who had been involved in the campaign.

Romney's apparently optimistic expectation on November 6 was indicated by his failure to prepare a concession speech until the eleventh hour. One campaign advisor later suggested the Republican "was shellshocked" by the result (Jan Crawford, "Adviser: Romney 'shellshocked' by loss," *CBS News*, November 8, 2012, accessed July 6, 2013 from http://www.cbsnews.com/8301-250_162-57547239/adviser-romney-shellshocked-by-loss). "There's nothing worse than when you think you're going to win, and you don't," said another advisor. "It was like a sucker punch" (Jan Crawford, "Adviser: Romney 'shellshocked' by loss"). How could the Romney pollsters have so grossly miscalculated the race? In an analysis published in the *New Republic*, Neil Newhouse, the campaign's chief pollster, discussed its final internal polling numbers for seven key states. The biggest flaw, Newhouse claimed, was misjudging the demographics of the electorate – non-white and young voters having shown up in numbers they didn't expect. Another problem was campaign pollsters had counted on the momentum they were supposedly gaining in the period after Romney's numbers had "stalled out" during Hurricane Sandy: "We thought we had in the last 72 hours of campaign ... made up some ground from the challenging messaging period during the hurricane" (Noam Scheiber, "The Internal Polls That Made Mitt Romney Think He'd Win," *The New Republic*, November 30, 2012, accessed July 6, 2013 from http://www.newrepublic.com/blog/plank/110597/exclusive-the-polls-made-mitt-romney-think-hed-win). While such a post-hoc mea culpa needs to be taken with a grain of salt, Nate Silver has suggested that errors of this kind may be endemic to partisan polling: "My database of campaign polls released to the public in United States House races found that they were about six points more favorable to their candidate than independent surveys on average – and that they were typically less accurate in the end." Silver's analysis of the seven state polls Newhouse released to the *New Republic* revealed an average bias of nearly five percentage points. Aside from any technical problems, Silver observed that insider polls for trailing campaigns may often be "fooling themselves": "A pollster ... may worry about harming the morale of the candidate or the campaign if he delivers bad news. Or he may be worried that the campaign will no longer be interested in his services if the candidate feels the race is hopeless. Groupthink and confirmation bias are also risks in any organization, particularly under the stress of the end stages of a political campaign" (Nate Silver, "When Internal Polls Mislead, a Whole Campaign May Be to Blame," *New York Times* (*FiveThirtyEight*), December 1, 2012, accessed July 6, 2013 from http://fivethirtyeight.blogs.nytimes.

com/2012/12/01/when-internal-polls-mislead-a-whole-campaign-may-be-to-blame/). These observations may themselves have been self-serving, of course, justifying Silver's own status as an independent, non-partisan observer who actually does not himself engage in polling. It strains credibility that insider polling would risk undermining the potential for a candidate's recuperative strategies by making falsely optimistic readings of campaign performances that failed to connect.

In its own post-election report, the Obama campaign's analytics department claimed, in fact, that it did vastly better than the best of the various poll aggregators, among them Nate Silver's *FiveThirtyEight*, as well as the Romney team. Their proprietary model, code-named "Golden," ran 62,000 simulations of the election daily. They asserted that it was not only more accurate but more accurate earlier in the race. According to the report, in battleground states, the Obama team "proved to be more than twice as accurate as RealClearPolitics' forecast, twice as accurate as Pollster.com's forecast, 58% more accurate than TalkingPointsMemo's forecast & 42% more accurate than Nate Silver's forecast" (Joshua Green, "Obama Campaign Says It Was 42 Percent More Accurate Than Nate Silver," *Bloomberg Businessweek*, June 6, 2013, accessed July 6, 2013 from http://www.businessweek.com/articles/2013-06-06/obama-campaign-says-it-was-42-percent-more-accurate-than-nate-silver).

65 Nate Silver, "Oct. 22: Ohio Has 50-50 Chance of Deciding Election," *New York Times* (*FiveThirtyEight*), October 23, 2012, accessed July 6, 2013 from http://fivethirtyeight.blogs.nytimes.com/2012/10/23/oct-22-ohio-has-50-50-chance-of-deciding-election/.

66 In contrast, the *FiveThirtyEight* prediction model had shown Obama with a 75 percent chance of winning Ohio at this point, chances that rose to about 80 percent by November 1 (Nate Silver, "Oct. 25: The State of the States," *New York Times* (*FiveThirtyEight*), October 26, 2012, accessed July 6, 2013 from http://fivethirtyeight.blogs.nytimes.com/2012/10/26/oct-25-the-state-of-the-states/; Nate Silver, "Oct. 31: Obama's Electoral College 'Firewall' Holding in Polls," *New York Times* (*FiveThirtyEight*), November 1, 2012, accessed July 6, 2013 from http://fivethirtyeight.blogs.nytimes.com/2012/11/01/oct-31-obamas-electoral-college-firewall-holding-in-polls/).

67 Jeff Zeleny and Jim Rutenberg, "In Final Days of the Race, Fighting County by County," *New York Times*, October 27, 2012, accessed July 6, 2013 from http://www.nytimes.com/2012/10/28/us/politics/in-final-days-of-presidential-election-fighting-county-by-county.html.

68 "Who Will Do More?" *YouTube*, posted by mittromney on October 28, 2012, accessed July 6, 2013 from http://www.youtube.com/watc h?v=VQ8P04q6jqE&feature=plcp.

69 Gualberto Ranieri, "Jeep in China," *Chrysler*, October 25, 2012, accessed July 6, 2013 from http://blog.chryslerllc.com/blog.do?id= 1932&p=entry.

70 Sergio Marchionne, "Message From Sergio Marchionne Regarding Jeep Production," *Chrysler*, October 30, 2012, accessed July 6, 2013 from http://blog.chryslergroupllc.com/entry/1950/message_from_ser gio_marchionne_regarding_jeep_production.

71 Mitt Romney, "Let Detroit Go Bankrupt," *New York Times*, November 18, 2008, accessed June 23, 2013 from http://www. nytimes.com/2008/11/19/opinion/19romney.html.

72 "Collapse – Obama for America TV Ad," *YouTube*, posted by BarackObamadotcom on October 29, 2012, accessed July 6, 2013 from http://www.youtube.com/watch?v=7iE5wBfM1LQ.

73 Ali Weinberg, "Obama slams Romney for Jeep ad in Ohio," *First Read on NBCNEWS.com*, November 2, 2012, accessed July 6, 2013 from http://firstread.nbcnews.com/_news/2012/11/02/14882672-ob ama-slams-romney-for-jeep-ad-in-ohio?lite.

74 Nate Silver, "Nov. 1: The Simple Case for Saying Obama Is the Favorite," *New York Times* (*FiveThirtyEight*), November 2, 2012, accessed July 6, 2013 from http://fivethirtyeight.blogs.nytimes. com/2012/11/02/nov-1-the-simple-case-for-saying-obama-is-the-favorite/.

75 Sam Wang, "Landfall," *Princeton Election Consortium*, October 27, 2012, accessed July 6, 2013 from http://election.princeton. edu/2012/10/27/landfall/.

76 Roger Cohen, "America's Gender Divide," *New York Times*, November 1, 2012, accessed July 6, 2013 from http://www.nytimes. com/2012/11/02/opinion/roger-cohen-americas-gender-divide. html. Just days prior, Red State's polling analyst Dan McLaughlin had declared "Barack Obama is toast," presenting a slew of historical polling data about Independents that supported such an assertion (Dan McLaughlin, "Why I Think Obama is Toast," *Red State*, October 26, 2012, accessed July 7, 2013 from http://www. redstate.com/2012/10/26/why-i-think-obama-is-toast/). McLaughlin provided a detailed analysis of the differences between his and Nate Silver's models, again focusing on the need to take historical data into serious consideration: "I stand by the view that a mechanical reading of polling averages is an inadequate basis to project an event unprecedented in American history: the re-election of a sitting president without a clear-cut victory in the national popular vote"

(Dan McLaughlin, "On Polling Models, Skewed & Unskewed," *Red State*, October 31, 2012, accessed July 7, 2013 from http://www. redstate.com/2012/10/31/on-polling-models-skewed-unskewed/). But as McLaughlin felt compelled to acknowledge after the race, "Sometimes, It Really Is Different This Time," devoting three long columns to explaining how his predictions could have gone so terribly wrong (Dan McLaughlin, "Sometimes, It Really Is Different This Time – A Polling Post-Mortem (Part I of III): The State Poll Averages Were Right," *Red State*, November 7, 2012, accessed July 7, 2013 from http://www.redstate.com/2012/11/14/sometimes-it-really-is-dif ferent-this-time-a-polling-post-mortem-part-i-of-iii/).

77 Janet Hook and Danny Yadron, "Sandy Spurs Campaigns to Shift Plans," *Wall Street Journal*, October 29, 2012, accessed July 6, 2013 from http://online.wsj.com/article/SB1000142405297020388070457 8086580384854940.html.

78 Leftist commentators claimed, nonetheless, that Romney remained partisan in his response. Rachel Maddow of MSNBC lambasted Romney for returning to the campaign trail so quickly and called the storm relief event a "blatant photo-op" ("Rachel Maddow To Mitt Romney: Hurricane Sandy 'Is A Real Disaster. This Is Not A Plot In A Sitcom' (VIDEO)," *HuffPost Media*, November 1, 2012, accessed July 6, 2013 from http://www.huffingtonpost.com/2012/11/01/rachel-maddow-video_n_2056211.html).

79 "Chris Christie's epic takedown of President Obama in Virginia," *YouTube*, posted by Chris Spiering on October 22, 2012, accessed July 6, 2013 from http://www.youtube.com/watch?v=Yxi-ZfD8uhM.

80 Kate Zernike, "One Result of Hurricane: Bipartisanship Flows," *New York Times*, October 31, 2012, accessed July 6, 2013 from http://www.nytimes.com/2012/11/01/nyregion/in-stunning-about-face-chris-christie-heaps-praise-on-obama.html.

81 Kate Zernike, "One Result of Hurricane: Bipartisanship Flows."

82 Raymond Hernandez, "Bloomberg Backs Obama, Citing Fallout From Storm," *New York Times*, November 1, 2013, accessed July 6, 2013 from http://www.nytimes.com/2012/11/02/nyregion/bloomb-erg-endorses-obama-saying-hurricane-sandy-affected-decision.html.

83 "Remarks by the President in Las Vegas, NV," *The White House President Barack Obama*, November 1, 2012, accessed July 6, 2013 from http://www.whitehouse.gov/the-press-office/2012/11/01/remarks-president-las-vegas-nv.

84 Nate Silver, "Nov. 2: For Romney to Win, State Polls Must Be Statistically Biased," *New York Times* (*FiveThirtyEight*), November 3, 2012, accessed July 6, 2013 from http://fivethirtyeight. blogs.nytimes.com/2012/11/03/nov-2-for-romney-to-win-state

-polls-must-be-statistically-biased/. At this juncture, Sam Wang put Romney's chances at only 6 percent and predicted a 2.5 percent margin on the popular vote ("How likely is a popular-vote/electoral-vote mismatch?" *Princeton Election Consortium*, November 3, 2012, accessed July 6, 2013 from http://election.princeton.edu/2012/11/03/how-likely-is-a-popular-voteelectoral-vote-mismatch/#more-8258).

85 Nate Silver, "Nov. 5: Late Poll Gains for Obama Leave Romney With Longer Odds," *New York Times* (*FiveThirtyEight*), November 6, 2012, accessed July 6, 2013 from http://fivethirtyeight.blogs.nytimes.com/2012/11/06/nov-5-late-poll-gains-for-obama-leave-romney-with-longer-odds/. Exit polls reported by CNN indicated that 64 percent of voters considered the president's hurricane response in their vote, and of that group a solid majority (62 percent) voted for Obama ("President: Full Results").

86 Roger Cohen, "America's Gender Divide."

87 "Ohio Voters Weary of Election Promises," *Wall Street Journal Live*, October 26, 2012, accessed July 6, 2013 from http://live.wsj.com/video/ohio-voters-weary-of-election-promises/28C65E4D-53AA-4CD1-9FA1-8C4845E4C729.html#!28C65E4D-53AA-4CD1-9FA1-8C4845E4C729.

88 Colleen McCain Nelson, Neil King, Jr., and Arian Campo-Flores, "Nail-Biter in 3 Key Counties," *Wall Street Journal*, November 5, 2012, accessed July 6, 2013 from http://online.wsj.com/article/SB10001424052970204707104578093250914927498.html.

89 "Obama and Romney Are Deadlocked," *Wall Street Journal Live*, November 5, 2012, accessed July 6, 2013 from http://live.wsj.com/video/obama-and-romney-are-deadlocked/8CCB305D-83E9-47EA-999A-0357EA1E73DE.html#!8CCB305D-83E9-47EA-999A-0357EA1E73DE.

90 Gerald F. Seib, "Strategists See 'Myths' Emerging From Other Side," *Wall Street Journal* (*Washington Wire*), November 2, 2012, accessed July 6, 2013 from http://blogs.wsj.com/washwire/2012/11/02/strategists-see-myths-emerging-from-other-side/.

91 Gerald F. Seib, "Strategists See 'Myths' Emerging From Other Side."

92 Gerald F. Seib, "Strategists See 'Myths' Emerging From Other Side."

93 Garrett Haake, "Romney says he's the candidate of 'big change' while barnstorming Ohio," *First Read on NBCNEWS.com*, October 25, 2012, accessed July 6, 2013 from http://firstread.nbcnews.com/_news/2012/10/25/14697654-romney-says-hes-the-candidate-of-big-change-while-barnstorming-ohio?lite.

94 "Remarks by the President in Madison, WI," *The White House President Barack Obama*, November 5, 2012, accessed July 6,

2013 from http://www.whitehouse.gov/the-press-office/2012/11/05/
remarks-president-madison-wi.

Chapter 8   Demography, Money, and Social Media

1 Richard S. Dunham, "Obama wins re-election," *San Francisco
Chronicle*, November 7, 2012, accessed July 6, 2013 from http://
www.sfgate.com/politics/article/Obama-wins-re-election-4014681.
php#ixzz2VFAsttHE.

2 Chuck Todd, Mark Murray, Domenico Montanaro, and Brooke
Brower, "First Thoughts: Obama's demographic edge," *First Read
on NBCNEWS.com*, November 7, 2012, accessed July 6, 2013 from
http://firstread.nbcnews.com/_news/2012/11/07/14993875-first-
thoughts-obamas-demographic-edge?lite.

3 Nancy Benac and Connie Cass, "Correction: Changing Electorate
story (Face of US changing; elections to look different)," *AP*,
November 15, 2012, accessed July 6, 2013 from http://bigstory.
ap.org/article/face-us-changing-elections-look-different.

4 Jonathan Alter, *The Center Holds*, pp. 269–281.

5 Susan Heavey, "Obama win shows demographic shifts working
against Republicans," *Reuters*, November 8, 2012, accessed July
6, 2013 from http://www.reuters.com/article/2012/11/08/us-usa-
campaign-diversity-new-idUSBRE8A70QK20121108. Republicans
exerted a great deal of effort to prevent increased voting turnout
among such groups, as well as among low-income and elderly voters.
From the 1990s, and especially intensely after the Democratic surge
in 2008, conservative political groups worked to enact what their
critics considered voter suppression laws – requiring a government-
issued photo ID or proof of citizenship to vote, cutting back on early
voting, eliminating Election Day registration, and other measures
that disproportionally affected groups of voters likely to vote for
a Democratic ticket. Obama's campaign, working with civil rights
groups such as the ACLU, largely neutralized this effort, and, indeed,
the publicity about it may have actually created a backlash that
intensified minority and youth voting. The Democratic anti-voter
suppression effort recruited a large staff of aggressive, highly trained
lawyers who filed a series of legal challenges in state and federal
courts. Early in the campaign season, in November, 2011, former
White House counsel Robert Bauer began organizing lawyers into
"voter-protection" teams that would monitor newly enacted voter
suppression laws as well as go into the field to help train voters and
poll watchers (Jonathan Weisman and Carol E. Lee, "Obama Aims
at Election Laws," *Wall Street Journal*, November 2, 2011, accessed

July 16, 2013 from http://online.wsj.com/article/SB1000142405297
02037075045770121213315643772.html).

The expanded ability to engage in voter suppression was due to
the increased influence Republicans wielded over state legislatures
and governorships – in America's federal system, voting is regulated
largely at the state level. Such increased influence was one largely
unnoticed result of the Democrats' 2010 midterm election debacle.
Another was the dramatic increase in Republican control over
the shaping of congressional voting districts. Coinciding with the
decadal census, redistricting occurs every 10 years, and the party that
wins control at the end of each decade has the power to rearrange
the boundaries of closely fought districts – "gerrymandering" them
– so as to maximize the chances of maintaining control in future
elections. In the 2012 election, Republican gerrymandering ensured
that, while Democrats nationally received millions more congressional votes, only a handful of congressional seats actually shifted
away from the Republican side.

6 Susan Heavey, "Obama win shows demographic shifts working
against Republicans."

7 Bill Marsh and Marjorie Connelly, "Groups Obama Won, Groups
Romney Won," New York Times, November 14, 2012, accessed
July 6, 2013 from http://www.nytimes.com/interactive/2012/11/10/
opinion/20101104_POLL-MARSH.html.

8 Although various exit polls showed that the support fell from 95 to
93 percent, an analysis by the New Republic revealed that turnout
among black voters may actually have been higher than in 2008 (Nate
Cohn, "What Black Turnout for Obama in 2012 Means for the GOP
in 2016," The New Republic, November 13, 2012, accessed July 6,
2013 from http://www.newrepublic.com/blog/electionate/110068/
the-overlooked-question-2016-the-future-black-turnout#).

9 Micah Cohen, "Gay Vote Proved a Boon for Obama," New York
Times, November 15, 2012, accessed July 6, 2013 from http://www.
nytimes.com/2012/11/16/us/politics/gay-vote-seen-as-crucial-in-
obamas-victory.html?hp.

10 In the tense final days of the 2012 campaign, the Obama campaign's
official website, Barackobama.com, distributed a get-out-the-vote
message from African American poet Maya Angelou to the millions
on its email list under the subject heading "Pretty or plain, heavy or
thin, gay or straight, poor or rich" (October 24, 2012):

> I am not writing to you as a black voter, or a woman voter, or as a
> voter who is over 70 years old and six feet tall. I am writing to you as
> a representative of this great country – as an American. It is your job to

vote. It is your responsibility, your right, and your privilege. You may be pretty or plain, heavy or thin, gay or straight, poor or rich. But remember this: In an election, every voice is equally powerful – don't underestimate your vote. Voting is the great equalizer. Voting has already begun in some states that President Obama needs to win. So please use this handy tool to make sure your friends in those key states know where to cast their ballot. You will be doing them a great favor ... As a country, we can scarcely perceive the magnitude of our progress. My grandmother and my uncle experienced circumstances that would break your heart. When they went to vote, they were asked impossible questions like, "How many angels can dance on the head of a pin?" When they couldn't answer, they couldn't vote. I once debated with the Rev. Martin Luther King Jr. about whether an African American would ever be elected president. He believed it would happen within the next 40 years at the time – I believed it would never happen within my lifetime. I have never been happier to have been proven wrong. And since President Barack Obama's historic election, we've moved forward in courageous and beautiful ways. More students can afford college, and more families have access to affordable health insurance. Women have greater opportunities to get equal pay for equal work. Yet as Rev. King wrote, "All progress is precarious." So don't sit on the sidelines. Don't hesitate. Don't have any regrets. Vote. Go, rise up, and let your friends and family in early vote states know where they can vote today. We must make our voices heard ... Your vote is not only important. It's imperative.

11 Joel Benenson, "Values, Not Demographics, Won the Election," *New York Times*, November 7, 2012, accessed July 6, 2013 from http://www.nytimes.com/2012/11/08/opinion/obama-won-on-values-not-demographics.html.

12 And it is notable that, in some of these 10 elections, certain white Democratic candidates received less of the white vote than Obama did. For example, Walter Mondale received only 34 percent in 1984. Domenico Montanaro, "Obama performance with white voters on par with other Democrats," *First Read on NBCNEWS.com*, November 19, 2012, accessed July 6, 2013 from http://firstread.nbcnews.com/_news/2012/11/19/15282553-obama-performance-with-white-voters-on-par-with-other-democrats?lite.

13 "Remarks by the President at the NALEO Annual Conference," *The White House President Barack Obama*, June 22, 2012, accessed September 18, 2013 from http://www.whitehouse.gov/the-press-office/2012/06/22/remarks-president-naleo-annual-conference.

14 "Un mensaje especial para la comunidad latina del Presidente Obama," *YouTube*, posted by BarackObamadotcom on November

3, 2012, accessed September 18, 2013 from http://www.youtube.com/watch?v=JT2LhMfe7lM.

15 Emily Deruy, "Spanish-Language Political Ad Money Just a Drop in the Bucket," *ABC News Univision*, November 16, 2012, accessed September 18, 2013 from http://abcnews.go.com/ABC_Univision/Politics/obama-camp-spent-spanish-language-ads/story?id=17741497.

16 "Chávez Por Obama," *YouTube*, posted by mittromney on November 1, 2012, accessed September 18, 2013 from http://www.youtube.com/watch?v=e-csfB8XRcw.

17 "Juntos," *YouTube*, posted by mittromney on August 28, 2012, accessed September 18, 2013 from http://www.youtube.com/watch?v=uqbWL-YYZvE.

18 "Remarks by the President and the First Lady at International Women's Day Reception," *The White House President Barack Obama*, March 8, 2010, accessed September 18, 2013 from http://www.whitehouse.gov/the-press-office/remarks-president-and-first-lady-international-womens-day-reception.

19 Valerie Strauss, "Obama's Barnard commencement speech – text," *Washington Post*, May 14, 2012, accessed September 18, 2013 from http://www.washingtonpost.com/blogs/answer-sheet/post/obamas-barnard-commencement-speech--text/2012/05/14/gIQAnZtPPU_blog.html.

20 "Remarks by the President at the LGBT Pride Month Reception," *The White House President Barack Obama*, June 15, 2012, accessed September 18, 2013 from http://www.whitehouse.gov/the-press-office/2012/06/15/remarks-president-lgbt-pride-month-reception.

21 "Remarks by the First Lady at the Congressional Black Caucus Gala," *The White House President Barack Obama*, September 23, 2012, accessed September 18, 2013 from http://www.whitehouse.gov/the-press-office/2012/09/23/remarks-first-lady-congressional-black-caucus-gala.

22 "'Important' – Obama for America TV Ad," *YouTube*, posted by BarackObamadotcom on August 4, 2012, accessed September 18, 2013 from http://www.youtube.com/watch?v=0YhDQJU1NlE.

23 "Decision – Obama for America TV Ad," *YouTube*, posted by BarackObamadotcom on October 12, 2012, accessed September 18, 2013 from http://www.youtube.com/watch?v=1eQGoQSOOM4.

24 "What He'll Do – Obama for America TV Ad," *YouTube*, posted by BarackObamadotcom on October 24, 2012, accessed September 18, 2013 from http://www.youtube.com/watch?v=P7QPLeGlEKw.

25 See, for example, "'Wingnuts' and President Obama: A socialist? A Muslim? Anti-American? The Anti-Christ? Large minorities of

Americans hold some remarkable opinions," *Harris Interactive*,
March 24, 2010, accessed July 6, 2013 from http://www.harrisinter-
active.com/NewsRoom/HarrisPolls/tabid/447/ctl/ReadCustom%20
Default/mid/1508/ArticleId/223/Default.aspx; Josh Gerstein, "Poll:
46% of GOP thinks Obama's Muslim," *Politico*, August 19, 2010,
accessed July 6, 2013 from http://www.politico.com/blogs/josh
gerstein/0810/Poll_46_of_GOP_thinks_Obamas_Muslim.html; and
"Little Voter Discomfort with Romney's Mormon Religion: Only
About Half Identify Obama as Christian," *The Pew Forum on
Religion & Public Life*, July 26, 2012, accessed July 6, 2013 from
http://www.pewforum.org/Politics-and-Elections/2012-romney-
mormonism-obamas-religion.aspx.
26 Stephanie Condon, "Poll: One in four Americans think Obama
was not born in U.S.," *CBS News*, April 21, 2011, accessed July 6,
2013 from http://www.cbsnews.com/8301-503544_162-20056061-
503544.html.
27 Tom Jensen, "Romney and the Birthers," *Public Policy Polling*,
February 15, 2011, accessed July 6, 2013 from http://publicpolicy
polling.blogspot.cz/2011/02/romney-and-birthers.html.
28 Alexander Burns, "Romney makes birth certificate joke," *Politico*,
August 24, 2012, accessed June 24, 2013 from http://www.politico.
com/blogs/burns-haberman/2012/08/romney-makes-birth-certifi
cate-joke-133091.html.
29 When Obama campaign operatives and activists spoke about their
determination to rebuild the kind of electoral coalition that had
once allowed liberals to become president, they emphasized broad
solidarity over demographic particularity, whatever their personal
ideologies or their identification with the interests or identities of
marginalized groups. John Halpin and Ruy Teixeira, for example,
are political intellectuals and strategists working at the Committee
for American Progress, an influential liberal Washington think-tank
that formed after the Clinton presidency and exercised significant
influence during Obama's first term and last campaign. Days after
Obama's re-election, they wrote of Obama's "Progressive Coalition"
as a "multi-racial, multi-ethnic, non-class coalition in support of an
active government that supports freedom, opportunity, and security
for all" (Ruy Teixeira and John Halpin, "The Return of the Obama
Coalition," *Center for American Progress*, November 8, 2012,
accessed September 7, 2013 from http://www.americanprogress.org/
issues/progressive-movement/news/2012/11/08/44348/the-return-
of-the-obama-coalition/). Elaborating on their analysis one month
later, Teixeira and Halpin offered two reasons for the president's
success, one "demographic shifts," the other "ideological shift in the

American electorate" (Ruy Teixeira and John Halpin, "The Obama Coalition in the 2012 Election and Beyond," *Center for American Progress*, December 4, 2012, accessed September 7, 2013 from http://www.americanprogress.org/issues/progressive-movement/report/2012/12/04/46664/the-obama-coalition-in-the-2012-election-and-beyond/). In other words, demographic status does not determine electoral politics. The political culture of demographically demarcated audiences needs to be molded, pushed to the left or the right. The people responsible for creating such ideological shifts are the political performers and their campaign teams.

30 Kimberly A. Strassel, "Four Little Words."

31 Jim Rutenberg and Jeff Zeleny, "Obama Mines for Voters With High-Tech Tools," *New York Times*, March 8, 2012, accessed July 6, 2013 from http://www.nytimes.com/2012/03/08/us/politics/obama-campaigns-vast-effort-to-re-enlist-08-supporters.html.

32 Journalist and media researcher Richard Parker described the phenomenon in a column for the *New York Times*: "The 50.5 million Hispanics in the country have higher usage rates of mobile and social media than Anglos. African Americans and Hispanics have adopted Twitter at faster rates than whites or Anglos ... More than three in five women who are of African American, Hispanic or Asian-American had a smartphone in 2011, compared to just one in three white women, according to Nielsen" (Richard Parker, "Social and Anti-Social Media," *New York Times* (*Campaign Stops*), November 15, 2013, accessed July 6, 2013 from http://campaignstops.blogs.nytimes.com/2012/11/15/social-and-anti-social-media/).

33 This figure represented more than two-and-a-half times as many as Romney's 12.1 million followers (Micah L. Sifry, "Presidential Campaign 2012, By the Numbers," *Tech President*, November 26, 2012, accessed July 6, 2013 from http://techpresident.com/news/23178/presidential-campaign-2012-numbers). Four days after the election, media were abuzz with the fact that Romney was losing Facebook fans at the rate of 847 per hour. While Obama had actually gained 804,479, Romney had lost 55,025 (Kevin Collier, "Mitt Romney Is Losing 847 Facebook Friends Per Hour," *Mashable*, November 10, 2012, accessed July 14, 2013 from http://mashable.com/2012/11/10/mitt-romney-is-losing-847-facebook-friends-per-hour/).

34 "Social Media Election," *Open Site*, October 11, 2012, accessed July 6, 2013 from http://open-site.org/blog/social-media-election/.

35 Jana Kasperkevic, "The Tweetelection: Obama had more than just the ground game in his favor," *SFGate* (*Politics*), November 7, 2012, accessed July 14, 2013 from http://blog.sfgate.com/

nov05election/2012/11/07/the-tweetelection-obama-had-more-than-just-the-ground-game-in-his-favor/.

36 Francis Bea, "Election night 2012 by the social media numbers," *Digital Trends*, November 7, 2012, accessed July 6, 2013 from http://www.digitaltrends.com/social-media/election-night-2012-by-the-social-media-numbers/#ixzz2NWXhxsQj.

37 Alex Fitzpatrick, "So Did Social Media 'Predict' the Election?" *Mashable*, November 8, 2013, accessed July 6, 2013 from http://mashable.com/2012/11/07/social-media-election/.

38 "Obama and Romney: Who's Using Media Better?" *Wall Street Journal Live*, May 25, 2012, accessed July 6, 2013 from http://live.wsj.com/video/obama-and-romney-whos-using-media-better/BA665A3A-8D37-4F13-B1C8-E8F7AFBA24AD.html#!BA665A3A-8D37-4F13-B1C8-E8F7AFBA24AD.

39 Jonathan Alter, *The Center Holds*, p. 89.

40 Paul Blumenthal, "Obama Ground Game: State Parties Flush With Cash In Swing States," *HuffPost Politics*, October 24, 2012, accessed July 6, 2013 from http://www.huffingtonpost.com/2012/10/24/obama-ground-game-swing-states_n_2009600.html.

41 "President Obama: 'I'm Really Proud of All of You,'" *YouTube*, posted by BarackObamadotcom on November 8, 2012, accessed July 6, 2013 from http://www.youtube.com/watch?v=pBK2rfZt32g.

42 See the Maya Angelou email in note 10 above.

43 Mary, "A look back at the campaign in numbers," *Organizing for America*, November 23, 2012, accessed July 6, 2013 from http://www.barackobama.com/news/entry/a-look-back-at-the-campaign-in-numbers.

44 John Dickerson, "How To Run a Killer Campaign: The president's campaign manager explains how the Obama campaign did it," *Slate*, November 15, 2012, accessed July 6, 2013 from http://www.slate.com/articles/news_and_politics/politics/2012/11/jim_messina_offers_his_tips_on_how_barack_obama_s_campaign_team_beat_mitt.single.html.

45 Jim Messina proudly stated from the onset, "We are going to measure every single thing in this campaign." He hired number-crunchers on a massive scale, five times that of the 2008 campaign, headed by "chief scientist" Rayid Ghani, an expert in analytics, machine learning, and data. While their exact operational details remained secret – "They are our nuclear codes," campaign spokesman Ben LaBolt quipped – (Michael Scherer, "Inside the Secret World of the Data Crunchers Who Helped Obama Win," *TIME Magazine*, November 7, 2012, accessed July 16, 2013 from http://swampland.

time.com/2012/11/07/inside-the-secret-world-of-quants-and-data-crunchers-who-helped-obama-win/#ixzz2VFWhpl8J), some impressive information about the highly publicized "Narwhal project" was available. Tomi Ahonen, an influential mobile and media consultant, described it as follows: "[Narwhal] is the biggest election-related voter list, supporter database and voting support system ever made. It cost over $100 million to produce, and employed over 120 engineers, programmers and mathematicians who worked on the project for more than a year. Its database covered over 175 million voters and massive amounts of data for real time use" (Tomi T. Ahonen, "The Definitive Article on Numbers and Performance of Narwhal vs Orca – Obama vs Romney – Datamining and voter activation in 2012 US election," *Communities Dominate Brands*, December 6, 2012, accessed July 16, 2013 from http://communities-dominate. blogs.com/brands/2012/12/the-definitive-article-on-numbers-and-performance-of-narwhal-vs-orca-obama-vs-romney-datamining-and-.html). The important point, however, is that all this sophisticated technology was used simply to make the one-to-one contacts of field organizers and volunteers more likely to be effective, by making it more likely they would be facing somebody who – through something they had filled out in the previous decade, something they had done, something they had bought – was at least slightly likely to be persuadable. In other words, the millions of dollars in research and computing were employed to make it more likely that performative fusion would take place.

46 Robert Hall, "The 2012 Election: 'It's the Relationship, Stupid,'" *HuffPost Politics*, December 12, 2012, accessed July 6, 2013 from http://www.huffingtonpost.com/robert-hall/the-2012-election-its-the_b_2278945.html. A noted author, consultant, and speaker, Robert Hall was cofounder and CEO of a 200-person relationship management firm with offices in the US, Canada, Latin America, the UK, South Africa, and Australia. He consulted for 20-plus years with major corporations about their connections with customers and employees.

47 Mitch Stewart, Jeremy Bird, and Marlon Marshall, "Brick-by-Brick: Building a Ground Game for 270," *Organizing for Action*, November 3, 2012, accessed July 6, 2013 from http://www.barackobama.com/news/entry/brick-by-brick-building-a-ground-game-for-270/.

48 Robert Hall, "The 2012 Election."

49 Michael Scherer, "Friended: How the Obama Campaign Connected with Young Voters. Social networks are transforming the way campaigns are conducted," *TIME Magazine*, November 20, 2012, accessed July 6, 2013 from http://swampland.time.com/2012/11/20/friended-how-the-obama-campaign-connected-with-young-vot

ers/#ixzz2VRf8NXJN. The other important aspect of targeted sharing is that it allowed the campaign to court a demographic that had no listed phone number – an estimated half of its target swing state voters under 29. It was able to reach about 85 percent of this group of voters through the uploaded Facebook friend lists (Michael Scherer, "Friended").

50 Michael Scherer, "Friended: How the Obama Campaign Connected with Young Voters."

51 Michael D. Shear, "Obama Campaign Releases iPhone App for Canvassing," *New York Times* (*The Caucus*), July 31, 2012, accessed July 6, 2013 from http://thecaucus.blogs.nytimes.com/2012/07/31/obama-campaign-releases-iphone-app-for-canvassing/.

52 Nate Silver, "Did Democrats Get Lucky in the Electoral College?" *New York Times* (*FiveThirtyEight*), February 26, 2013, accessed July 6, 2013 from http://fivethirtyeight.blogs.nytimes.com/2013/02/26/did-democrats-get-lucky-in-the-electoral-college/.

53 Tim Dickinson, "President Obama's Six Keys to Victory: Inside the multicultural, center-left coalition that ensured four more years," *Rolling Stone*, November 7, 2012, accessed July 6, 2013 from http://www.rollingstone.com/politics/news/how-president-obama-beat-mitt-romney-20121107.

54 Kenneth P. Vogel, Dave Levinthal, and Tarini Parti, "Barack Obama, Mitt Romney both topped $1 billion in 2012," *Politico*, December 7, 2012, accessed June 23, 2013 from http://www.politico.com/story/2012/12/barack-obama-mitt-romney-both-topped-1-billion-in-2012-84737.html.

55 Our contextualization of demography-as-destiny claims relates to similar, if more directly materialist arguments for the centrality of "interest" to struggles for political power. There has not been much discussion in this book of the *interests* of different individuals and groups. In our view, such interests come into electoral struggles only as they are perceived and mobilized by politicians. "Raw" or latent interests – demographic positionings along economic, racial, gender, ethnic, sexual, regional, generational, and sexual lines – crystallize into manifest interests only as they are filtered through cultural discourses and their reception. The extraordinary fluidity of electoral politics is the result of the shifting back and forth of allegiances of demographic/interest group members who perceive their interests differently at one time or another depending on how various cultural constructions stick.

56 Michael Luo, "Money Talks Louder Than Ever in Midterms," *New York Times*, October 7, 2010, accessed July 6, 2013 from http://www.nytimes.com/2010/10/08/us/politics/08donate.html.

57 Indeed, there was considerable worry over funds, especially at the beginning of the campaign, before Obama had given the Priorities USA Action super PAC his blessing in February, 2012. Yet, each moment of anxiety produced an immediate acceleration of fundraising, as the campaign drew upon the cultural commitment of the grass roots. The following text of an email from campaign manager Jim Messina, sent in July, 2012, is described by Jeff Emanuel, of the conservative Red State blog, as "pure, sweet desperation":

> Jeff –
> Romney and the Republicans announced yesterday that they brought in more than $100 million in June.
> For context, that's about what we raised in April and May combined.
> We're still tallying our own numbers, but his means their gap is getting wider, and if it continues at this pace, it could cost us the election.
> If everyone who's been waiting to give pitches in $3 or more today, we can start reversing this trend in just a few hours.
> Please do your part – make a donation of $3 or more right now.
> One hundred million is alarming enough, but it doesn't even include the millions pouring into pro-Romney super PACs – or the fact that, unlike four years ago, it's perfectly legal for the Koch brothers, Sheldon Adelson, Karl Rove, and anonymous billionaires to funnel unlimited money into attacking President Obama in critical battleground states.
> I'm proud of the way we build this organization. Through the primaries, more than three-quarters of our donations were from people giving less than $1,000. Meanwhile, in that same period, Mitt Romney's campaign raised three-quarters of its money from people giving $1,000 or more.
> If we don't take this seriously now, we risk finding ourselves at a point where there is too much ground to make up.
> We need to do something about it. Today.
> Please donate $3 or more:
> https://donate.barackobama.com/Close-the-Gap
> More to come.
> (Jeff Emanuel, "Obama's 'billion dollar campaign' getting increasingly desperate for cash," *Red State*, July 6, 2012, accessed July 15, 2013 from http://www.redstate.com/jeff_emanuel/2012/07/06/is-the-billion-dollar-campaign-about-to-go-out-like-a-sucker/.)

But such missives proved effective, with Obama finally outpacing Romney in donations for the first time in months, raising $114 million in August, as compared to $75 million in June and $71 million in July. And many (more than a third) were new donors:

317,954 of the 1,170,000 people who gave in August had not yet contributed this election season (Arielle Hawkins, "Obama out-raises Romney for first time in months," *CNN (political ticker...)*, September 10, 2012, accessed July 15, 2013 from http://political-ticker.blogs.cnn.com/2012/09/10/obama-outraises-romney-for-first-time-in-months/).

58 In the end, the Republican super PACs far outspent the Democrats in Election 2012 – by nearly three-and-a-half times ("General election outside spending by candidate backed, 2011–12," *Sunlight Foundation Reporting Group* April 11, 2013, accessed July 15, 2013 from http://reporting.sunlightfoundation.com/outside-spending-2012/by-spending/). But the latter spent their funds much more effectively. As Paul Blumenthal of the *Huffington Post* put it: "As it turns out, you can't buy a different electorate, or a better candidate, no matter how much money you throw at it" (Paul Blumenthal, "Super PACs, Outside Money Influenced, But Didn't Buy The 2012 Election," *The Huffington Post*, November 7, 2012, accessed July 15, 2013 from http://www.huffingtonpost.com/2012/11/07/super-pacs-2012-election-outside-money_n_2087040.html). An NBC News investigation into Republican super PAC spending announced, "Karl Rove's Election Debacle," and cited Donald Trump's tweet: "Congrats to @KarlRove on blowing $400 million cycle. Every race @CrossroadsGPS ran ads in, the Republicans lost. What a waste of money" (Michael Isikoff, "Karl Rove's election debacle: Super PAC's spending was nearly for naught," *NBC News Investigations*, November 8, 2012, accessed July 15, 2013 from http://investiga tions.nbcnews.com/_news/2012/11/08/15007504-karl-roves-el ection-debacle-super-pacs-spending-was-nearly-for-naught?lite). The Sunlight Foundation reported a mere 1.29 percent "return on invest-ment" for American Crossroads, Rove's super PAC (Lindsay Young, "Outside spenders' return on investment," *Sunlight Foundation Reporting Group*, December 18, 2012, accessed July 15, 2013 from http://reporting.sunlightfoundation.com/2012/return_on_invest ment/).

59 The *Wall Street Journal* reported, "underscoring the magnitude of the reversal," that Goldman had been "the No. 1 source of cam-paign cash to Democrats among companies during the 23 years the Center for Responsive Politics has been collecting such data" (Liz Rappaport and Brody Mullins, "Goldman Turns Tables on Obama Campaign," *Wall Street Journal*, October 10, 2012, accessed June 24, 2013 from http://online.wsj.com/article/SB1000087239639044475 2504578024661927487192.html).

60 The funds donated by these organizations came from their

employees, members or owners and their immediate families, or the organizations' PACs. We cite these bundled donations as an indicator of the orientation of the flow of support ("Candidate Comparison: 2012 Presidential Candidates," *OpenSecrets.org; The Center for Responsive Politics*, as of March 25, 2013, accessed June 24, 2013 from https://www.opensecrets.org/pres12/head2head. php?ql3). Moreover, individual donations under $200 to the Obama campaign made up 67 percent of the total and just 14 percent gave the maximum of $2,500. The numbers for Romney were 26 percent and 47 percent respectively ("Contributions to Obama, Barack Through 12/31/2012," *Federal Election Commission*, n.d., accessed July 7, 2013 from http://www.fec.gov/disclosurep/pnational.do; "Contributions to Romney, Mitt Through 12/31/2012," *Federal Election Commission*, n.d., accessed July 7, 2013 from http://www. fec.gov/disclosurep/pnational.do).

Index